In Praise of Pedagogy

In Praise of Pedagogy

Poetry, Flash Fiction, and Essays on Composing

Edited by
Wendy Bishop
and
David Starkey

Foreword by
Ken Autrey

Calendar Islands Publishers
Portland, Maine

Calendar Islands Publishers LLC
477 Congress Street, Portland, Maine 04101

First published by Calendar Islands Publishers, 2000

ISBN 1-893056-08-2

Selection, Foreword, Introduction, and Afterword
Copyright © 2000 by Calendar Islands Publishers

All rights reserved. No part of this book may be reproduced in any form or by any means, except for brief quotation in a review or professional work, without permission in writing from Calendar Islands Publishers.

Library of Congress Cataloging-in-Publication Data on file

Design by Phillip Augusta

Printed in the United States of America
05 04 03 02 01 00   10 9 8 7 6 5 4 3 2 1

Table of Contents

Foreword by Ken Autrey — xi
   Spring Rice Field   xi

Introduction by Wendy Bishop — 1
   Jo'al   1
   When I was black—Jo'al Hill   4
   The True Story of Theme Heaven   5
   Cross-Cultural Genres   8
   Here in the New World   10
   First-Year Writing—Florida   12
   Homework   13
   I Send Poems   14
   How Does a Poem Start?   15
   Night Songs   16
   Workshop Memory   17
   Othering   19

Part I: From and For Classrooms
First Night of Class   Laura Apol — 23
The Poet Meets His Class in the
   Chemistry Lab   Ken Autrey — 24
tuesday 8:45   Joseph H. Ball — 25
The English Teacher's Bad Day   Grace Bauer — 26
Teaching Poetry: A Way to Grace
   the World?   Kelly Cherry — 27
Before Everything   Devan Cook — 29
Freshman Lit & Comp   Stephen Corey — 31

english 098 PHEBE DAVIDSON	32
Childbearing Hips ALLISON JOSEPH	33
Workshop Pantoum ALLISON JOSEPH	35
Open Letter to My Students KATHLEEN KIRK	36
Taking the World Literature Class Outside JANET MCCANN	38
Literacy: Or How I Ended Up at the Old Folks Home ANNE-MARIE OOMEN	40
Watching My Students Write ROBERT PARHAM	43
Flattened by Flattery TERRY RASMUSSEN	44
Nervouswork WILLIAM SNYDER, JR.	45
Preciousness of Imperfection WILLIAM SNYDER, JR.	46
There Are Miracles Extant In This World WILLIAM SNYDER, JR.	47
The Portuguese Princess Looks to the East THOMAS STEIN	48
The Big Up LARRY STRAUSS	50
Logical Fallacies ALISON TOWNSEND	52
Perspective PATRICIA VALDATA	54
Stone Dreams JANE ELKINGTON WOHL	55
Teaching Reading JANE ELKINGTON WOHL	57

Part II: *Language and the World*

The Dream of Teaching KEN AUTREY	61
The Scholar GRACE BAUER	62
Intro to Poetry STEVEN BAUER	63
The Death of Reading DARRELL FIKE	64
Windshield Vipers (Keeping Time) KATHERINE M. FISCHER	65
Wrestle Theory ALICE GEORGE	66
A Reading HOLLY IGLESIAS	68

Teaching in My Sleep   KATHLEEN KIRK   69
*Teacher Shot by Student, or The
    Risk of Overstatement*   KATHLEEN KIRK   70
Introduction to Poetry   SHANNON MARQUEZ MCGUIRE   71
Ignoring the Linguist   ROBERT PARHAM   73
Reading for the Blind   KARA PROVOST   74
The Teacher   TOM ROMANO   76
A Case for Literature   DARRELL G.H. SCHRAMM   77
Nostradamus in Heaven   SARAH SLOANE   78
Playground   KATE SONTAG   80

Part III: *Of Reading, Writing, Teaching, Being Taught*

Prepositions in Alabama   KEN AUTREY   83
Art Lesson   CRAIG CHALLENDER   84
Blizzard   CYNTHIA MILLER COFFEL   87
Art Elective   STEPHEN COREY   89
Chalk Dust and Urban Renewal   TRISTA CORNELIUS   93
my last glad summer   PHEBE DAVIDSON   95
Bar Mitzvah Lessons   MARVIN DIOGENES   96
Crescendo   KATHERINE M. FISCHER   97
My Bad   DOUGLAS GOETSCH   99
Puttyroot and Stopcock   DAVID GRAHAM   101
First Piano Teacher   AVA LEAVELL HAYMON   102
*After an Old Picture of
    School House Children*   WILL HOCHMAN   103
The Autobiography of Tulips   HOLLY IGLESIAS   104
Deep Blue   HOLLY IGLESIAS   105
Amphibians Have Feelings Too   GERALD LOCKLIN   107
Second Apartment, First-Year Teacher
    CLAUDIA MONPERE MCISAAC   108
Teachers' Lounge   BILL RANSOM   110

Rehabilitating Joseph Adams SCOTT SIMPSON	111
Spatial Relations LEONORA SMITH	115
"...Water and the Word Suicide" KATE SONTAG	117
Diction Lesson PATRICIA VALDATA	118

Part IV: *Advice and Observations*

Compulsion JANE BARNES	121
Flat Out JACQUELINE BRICE-FINCH	122
Advice to a Young Poet KELLY CHERRY	124
Reply HELEN DEGEN COHEN	125
Adjunct BROCK DETHIER	126
Not to Be BROCK DETHIER	127
Produce DARRELL FIKE	128
Wildflower Composition MELISSA GOLDTHWAITE	129
Just Guessing: A Little Lecture on Ambition DAVID GRAHAM	130
Creative Writing at Jefferson Correctional Institution AMORAK HUEY	131
Rules of Conduct: Colored *Elementary School, 1943* ALLISON JOSEPH	132
quo vadis, m.f.a.? GERALD LOCKLIN	133
Seven Fables of Teaching and Learning HANS OSTROM	134
Comma Splice WILLIAM M. RAMSEY	137
The Grammarian DARRELL G.H. SCHRAMM	138
The Trouble with Writing SARAH SLOANE	139
The Five Paragraph Essay LEONORA SMITH	140
Scenes from the "Teaching Moment" Lounge LYNNA WILLIAMS	142

Part V: *Memories of Our Children and Families Learning*

Beast on the Brink JANE BARNES	147
Geography Lessons GRACE BAUER	148

Table of Contents ix

Everything We Need DEVAN COOK	149
i'm very proud of her GERALD LOCKLIN	150
Academic Kids JANET MCCANN	152
Can You Predict the Past? Can You Remember the Future? JANET MCCANN	153
Becky's Mirror DEAN NEWMAN	154
Brains and Books DIANE PAYNE	156
Fish, Spring, Window LEONORA SMITH	158
A Rhetoric of Wood MICHAEL SPOONER	160
X DOYLE WESLEY WALLS	162
Roses and Tulips JANE ELKINGTON WOHL	164

Part VI: *Remembering Those Who Taught Us*

A Note About Allen Tate KELLY CHERRY	169
To an Ex-Student, On Learning She Is a World-Class Gymnast STEPHEN COREY	172
Mr. Howard GERALDINE DELUCA	173
Mystery and Manners MARVIN DIOGENES	175
For W. H. Auden and Alain Bombard SKIP EISIMINGER	177
Highlights DOUGLAS GOETSCH	178
Long Overdue Note to My College Professor Who Broke Down and Cried One Morning in 1974 While Teaching Yeats DAVID GRAHAM	180
Seminar SHANNON MARQUEZ MCGUIRE	182
The Physics Teacher ANNE-MARIE OOMEN	184
Sister Albert BILL RANSOM	186
All Hail Digredi ANGUS WOODWARD	188

Afterword: by David Starkey *The Art of Pedagogy/The Pedagogy of Art*	*191*
The Art of Pedagogy 191	
Instructions for Composing a Haiku 193	

Poems, Like Children 195
Buttons 196
*An Elderly Woman Falls Asleep
  at a Poetry Reading* 197
The Year My Poetry Became a Fad 199
The Pedagogy of Art 201

Contributors' Notes   *203*
Acknowledgments   *213*

Foreword

Several years ago, I was in my office working late at Hiroshima University, where I taught English for a year. Specifically, I was struggling with a poem that was turning into yet another vapid exploration of cross-cultural experience. The metaphors were getting tangled, and my computer was balking, so I walked out into the chilly Japanese evening and over to the library. Scanning the English language periodicals, I picked up the latest issue of *American Scholar*. The pages fell open to a poem, "Instructions for Composing a Haiku." Given the work I'd just turned away from, I found this a startling coincidence. My surprise turned to incredulity when I saw that its author was my former colleague, David Starkey. Eventually, perhaps the following day, I finished my poem:

Spring Rice Field

Basho's great haiku:
one frog leaps into a pond,
sound of a lifetime.

On a terraced hill north of Hiroshima,
water pours into a spring rice field
surrounded tonight by a world of frogs.
Air tilts with their trilling,
which rises and falls in waves.
Though I were at the water's edge,
leaning into the green smell
of newly-sprigged rice, listening
with all my heart, I could not hear
a lone splash amid the mating rabble.

It is not a night
for haiku, strand of wisdom
peeled from a still pond.

Whatever the quality of these sixteen lines, my riff on Basho, that moment in a faraway library confirmed my belief in the rhetoric of poetry and its power to forge assertions about pedagogy and art. David's poem, which reappears in his Afterword to this collection, provided for me less a haiku-like burst of insight than quick confirmation of a long-felt truth about teaching poetry and prose composition: Writing creatively about teaching matters as much as teaching creatively about writing.

My fortuitous discovery of David's poem under those circumstances was still on my mind when he, Wendy Bishop, and I began the conversation that led to a 1999 CCCC panel we called "Poems and Poets on Composing." The conversation, urged along by Peter Stillman and John C. Watson at Calendar Islands Publishers, has now culminated in this rich anthology of poetry, flash fiction, and essays.

As full of surprises as this volume is, it was inevitable that such a collection would emerge—and that Wendy and David would be its ideal midwives. Each has ardently advocated in print and in person the value of bringing together composition and creative writing pedagogy. In her introduction Wendy addresses the pervasive skepticism about this mix and enlists a number of her own poems in her case for the pedagogical and rhetorical power of poetry. *In Praise of Pedagogy*, as the title implies, is a celebration, but it embodies the rigorous principles that Wendy articulated in soliciting program proposals for CCCC in the year 2000: "Educating our imaginations does not mean we substitute flights of fancy for the hard work of finding solutions to old problems. It may mean, as it means for any learner, trying and not-at-first succeeding. Experimentation, the play of ideas, invention, essay-ing, all offer us necessary space to grow."

In his Afterword, David counters the academic bias against meta-poetry (or meta-writing of any sort), employing, like

Wendy, a number of poems in the process. In the introduction to his edited volume, *Teaching Writing Creatively*, David asks that we imagine a course in which students address "their own resistance and attraction to 'creative' writing in the composition class. They are then given choices about what and how to write that at first seem unimaginably liberating: narrative, collage, imitation, collaboration, even fiction and poetry. Their teachers, themselves writers, participate in the creativity and experimentation" (xvii). His own essay in that collection boldly advocates language poetry exercises in the composition classroom.

In recent years, the old connection between ars poetica and ars rhetorica has been reclaimed thanks in large measure to these two editors, as well a handful of others, such as Joseph Moxley and Mimi Schwartz, whose writing and editing have opposed the academic compartmentalization that too often artificially separates rhetoric, creative writing, and pedagogy. *In Praise of Pedagogy* provides the strongest possible confirmation of the richness that results when we think and write creatively about our lives in the classrooms, halls, offices, labs, and libraries where we spend our working days.

W. H. Auden famously asserted that "poetry makes nothing happen," but nearly four centuries earlier, Philip Sidney called poetry, "the first light-giver to ignorance." Judging from the work herein, Sidney may be closer to the truth. Whether or not the poems, essays, and flash fiction here make anything happen, they are filled with insights on the students, logical fallacies, assignments, comma splices, essays, lesson plans, coffee breaks, struggles, seminars, memorable teachers, and novels that occupy us, that inhabit us. They offer tributes, capture poignant moments, and recount anecdotes, but they also develop arguments, defend positions, and explain theories.

An unusual number of metaphors touched on or thoroughly elaborated in this collection derive from the natural world. The poetry and prose selections here are filled with growing things: a field of wheat, a snowy owl, a live oak tree, ginger root, moth wings, roses, red buds, melons. I don't think this is simply explained by the poet's instinctive attraction to organic images. This imagistic fecundity implies a collective attitude about teaching, an affirmation of the development that we so fervently want our students to experience and a doggedly positive outlook for our profession. Skepticism, uncertainty, even despair, are perennial occupational hazards for those of us who value language and respect its power. *In Praise of Pedagogy* provides reason for hope and presents a many-faceted argument for creatively exploring our teaching, for meta-writing about our composing, and for helping our students and colleagues see the value of both.

KEN AUTREY

Introduction

WENDY BISHOP

> Jo'al
>
> and the five senses, use them "concretely"
> but weirdly
> make lungs ring like brass bells
> make skin feel hot and foolish like caramel,
> make eyes track lucid questions in sky blue—
> guides to coax the day into formal
> shapes she's hesitant to use.
> Jo'al asks me, can she put metaphors
> in poetry? Can she use her own words
> like chitterlings and cornbread?
> Pushed back from a heavy desk,
> I see blocks of days,
> some for creating, some for composing.
> Then I say "yes." Yes.
> Southern fried and hamhocks steaming,
> naps, and plaits twisting patient hands.
> I share my mother's lost Norwegian
> farmlands and lilting syllables
> flattened, all rules followed.
> Jo'al listens between
> the messages. Thanks me.
> Her next poem, "When I Was
> Black," her best.

At an MLA conference many years ago and far far away (seemingly in another galaxy, given the time and teaching that have passed between then and now), I found myself making an uphill argument: that poetry can do more work than it has been allowed to do in the academy. It can argue; it can commemorate; it can explore, critique, and complicate our thinking. I had learned that by accident when I wrote my poem, above, addressed to Jo'al, a student who was confused about conflicting writing advice her composition and creative writing teachers were giving her that term.

This collection is in many ways the same argument written more boldly by high school and college writing and reading teachers across the country. Although such pieces can be difficult to write, as David Starkey notes in his closing essay to this book, and though I was chastised for writing them myself in my days as a creative writing student, I continue to marvel at the way creative writing about our teaching lives can lend insight and depth to that work, providing a journal of our journeys by underlining and pointing out the importance of particular events, crises, and turning points; events, crises, and turning points that may get lost in the plain-style of our expository prose on similar subjects.

David and I believe that reading these works will make you want to explore pedagogical themes yourself, that proof of a useful collection of writing is that it makes us want . . . to write.

More personally, subversion is my goal. I would like to see pedagogical poems and flash fictions and essays cited more often and explored and discussed more regularly. I would like to think that teachers are sharing their works with their classes and their families and non-academic communities. That they would do the former in order to encourage their students to write in service of exploring their own literacies. That they would do the latter in order to investigate the pejorative connotations nowadays associated with the term "occasional" verse. Consider the reversal: Sometimes a few words are worth a thousand pictures. As Devan Cook notes:

> I keep thinking about the Renaissance commonplace
> books of poetry that circulated, and how they are like

people e-mailing each other poems and setting up Web pages with their stuff. Nobody was thinking, "Great! I'm the Earl of Sidney, and I'm going to write the first sonnets in English and people are going to be kissing my butt for eons." (I like Sidney, actually.) No, he was thinking about being in love. This is my new thing: writing is contextual, localized, situated, and transitory. Actually, it's not my new thing—it's Derrida's old thing, but you know, it makes me feel better and helps me just enjoy writing this whatever-it-is right now, the person I am this minute . . . I think about Natalie Goldberg's idea of "mental writing" (the poem I write in my mind while walking around Lake Ella) being a different poem—specific for that time, place, and circumstance—than the one I write when I get home—even though I'm attempting (and constantly, constantly failing) to finish or take off from that earlier mental poem.

It surely couldn't harm a conference presentation or two or ten to be enlivened with a bow to the fine arts that such works represent, for encouraging writing and reading are the twin goals of our careful writing-and-reading-together-in-schools.

To make my point via personal testimony, I invite you on a stroll (like Devan's around Lake Ella) through my pedagogical creations with the understanding that I do this to champion the work we're sharing here and to call you back to your own writing. And because in doing this I can highlight some of the themes and approaches taken by the writers whose works you'll encounter in this book which results from a general call that was worded this way: "*In Praise of Pedagogy* will include poems and flash fictions on writing, teaching, reading, classroom environments, students, literacy, and related topics."

I believe that creative writing on such topics can help teachers:

1. solve problems
2. share understandings
3. deal with teaching conditions
4. observe: see better, more clearly, and more deeply
5. note, commemorate, save, and savor

6. critique
7. celebrate
8. poke fun, often at oneself, in productive ways
9. highlight contradictions
10. become better readers, writers, teachers
11. investigate and shed new light on issues
12. theorize and work out positions *[margin note: in this order???]*
13. argue and persuade

As I mentioned, "Jo'al" resulted from my need to understand a writing student, to solve the problem she posed in a conference one day when she asked me—seriously—if she was allowed to use metaphors in her poetry in poetry-writing class because her composition teacher was hammering home the point that she should avoid metaphors in her report writing. My poem, shared that term with Jo'al, allowed her to see how surprised I was that she was the subject of contradictory advice from two authorities, leading to confusion in both her writing classes. A veteran teacher now, I would expect this to happen. For the novice teacher I was then, Jo'al was both a student and a teaching problem that I needed to solve as much as she did. Her poem, mentioned in mine, appears here as part of our mutual sharing:

When I was black
Jo'al Hill

The clothing I wore was
clean, the language I
spoke was acceptable
the color of my eyes
were pretty, the naps in
my hair were unique,
the stutter in my voice
was natural, the
charcoal color of
my skin was a symbol
of pride.

> Cornbread was good
> Chitterlings were
> tasty
> Ham hocks were
> deepfried
> Southern Fried was
> Not KFC or Churches
> Chickens, but it
> was Mother's.
> Pig ears were
> considered dessert.
>
> I thought of black things,
> like stealing or cheating
> or lying, or beatings
> and even killing.
>
> Now I'm okay.   (Bishop 1998, 106)

Having been allowed to work through a teaching contradiction with Jo'al, I was better prepared to examine the often ludicrous physical and institutional teaching constraints that would be coming my way.

Writing to Deal with Teaching Conditions (and Sometimes Institutional Absurdity)

When I first arrived at Florida State University and began to direct the writing program there, we kept freshmen (they weren't yet first-year) writers' papers for one year after the students completed the course before destroying them; this was done, I learned, to try to keep the papers from being used again in other classes.

The True Story of Theme Heaven

> Before process,
> back during product,
> at the time of fraternity
> and sorority theme-files,

of look-alike five paragraph
full-thesesed, clear, coherent and unified
but god-awfully boring compare,
contrast, divide, classify, topoi-tried
pen-written contemplations,
theme heaven was called into being
behind a door on the top floor
of a tortuous English department
physical plant, often
remodeled into TA and adjunct faculty non-offices,
rabbit-warrened, maze-corridored,
a church of learning,
this edifice that course catalog
computers call the WMS BLDG.
To prevent plagiarism
of already borrowed thought,
themes were re-collected by their
rule-heavy assigners ("*no paragraph
without a thesis, never a conjunction
before a period, outline before you
think, awk, cs, ww, frag*").
Therefore,
sheaves of murmuring descriptions,
oceans of persuasion,
a universe of pure, untainted exposition,
collect each semester
for ritual remaindering
(and occasional rhetorical research)
while freshpersons pass on,
eons slip away, clichéd times change,
yet still themes accrue in theme heaven,
by unmodified rule.

Each year,
in unnoticed ritual,
the trash truck
backs smack up under a senior
professor's window.
High in theme heaven
sashes are raised
and bale after bale

after bale after bale—
words, lines, paragraphs, pages
of ephemeral focus, lost voice,
unachieved tone, missed transitions—
themes swan-dive, join a fluttering fall,
a non-angelic choir
of hostage thought,
plunges once again
and all at once
from theme heaven
to dumpster hell.

The solution of course was not to confiscate student texts but to design a curriculum that kept such recycling or plagiarism from occurring by asking each student to work on multiple drafts of their papers, to revise and review these texts with peers and teacher, and to collect all drafts and submit them for end-of-term review in a writing portfolio which was the student's own best representation of her written products. Then, we no longer had to clear theme heaven each year and shred the modal themes stacked heart-breakingly high therein. I could never pass that small locked windowless room without thinking almost fondly of that time of institutional absurdity. Theme Heaven has gone the way of the black metal Underwood typewriter (and the Selectric-wielding departmental manuscript typist) and the modal rhetoric and even of the poetry workshop that points all class members to works of dead white male poets, but it's good, I believe, to have such a reminder of it linger, tongue-in-cheek, into a century where every writer can own a personal paper shredder.

Writing to Observe: To See Better, More Clearly, More Deeply

It has never been particularly safe to praise pedagogy; often it's downright dangerous. In the last half of the twentieth century, college English Departments became sites where highest value was placed on *proven* literary texts and on the control of the same. Became sites that resisted popular art—art that makes money or satisfies the aesthetics of large populations—until it could be re-inscribed as valuable through American studies and cultural studies programs. Became sites that resisted collaboration for the way such practices challenged the primacy of solo authorship. In those preferences, many of our programs were poorly designed for beginners and for those with wide-ranging interests (*dilettantes* was the most pejorative term); I'm trying to reclaim *generalist* as a positive one—people like me who prefer to comb through and combine instead of distill down and winnow out. This was not a good pedagogical playing-field for those of dialects, languages, groups, beliefs, belongings other than those of the standard mid-twentieth-century English major.

"I yam what I yam. Affiliate (though I'll make it very hard to do so)—or go away" had to give way to "Who am I? And who are you? And what are we doing here together?" An interest in—a need for—pedagogy was brought to the fore by the increase of multi-cultural students in increasingly more multi-cultural America (and we'd do well to remember that these students arrived far ahead of multi-cultural scholarship).

Persons Before Positions would be my bumper sticker here: we can't know a person until we've explored, investigated, and inhabited some version of his or her perspective. A perfect vehicle for this, I argue, is the pedagogical poem or story.

Cross-Cultural Genres

> Here is an Eskimo ABC book. Here is Tununak graveyard, filled with snow, blown in shapes of animals moving just beneath the cold skin. Picket fence pierces like spearheads, herds life toward an Orthodox cross.
>
> Houses in a white on white landscape sit as square ships, antennae pointed toward outer space which doesn't exist in a land where "they deny planning." The universe exists, yet an elder's narrative seems, unfairly, a mouthful of glottal stops, remolding my conception of story—plot, tension, dramatic moment—I drift and slip into another

meaning system with Adam Fisher, nasal laugh and nasal laugh and nasal laugh.

We have no real patience for stories. We who "always talk about what's going to happen later" never stop to examine what is. She's young—just started having periods. Shimmies skinny slim hips, squeezes them into comfortable straight Wranglers, walks different but like her older brother, calls electricity to the ends of crackling black hair that she smoothes in hanks.

Silence is built into the land, pale off-tan grass, gathered Sundays after the traveling priest moves out of the village on a snow machine. Machine sputters and shrives silence then engulfs the Bering Sea while Adam Fisher tells a story, nasal laugh and nasal laugh and nasal laugh.

Things with hair stand out: musk ox, seal, men, women. Perspective is plotted by color of bronze skin and enlivened faces against muted palate of weathered buildings, steam of sweat houses, undergreen of tundra, far gray of airplane shadow.

"They are too indirect, too inexplicit. They don't make sense. They just leave without saying anything." In the Tununak graveyard, snow shifts shapes, graves fill, grass bows down, *A*s *B*s *C*s tussle with sea wind. They leave, they leave without saying anything.

This poem grew from an in-class cross-cultural awareness exercise designed by Carolyn Kremers, who asked a group of creative writers studying the teaching of creative writing to compare Anglo culture with Native Alaskan culture through the use of cultural assumption lists (for instance, "They [Anglos] always talk about what is going to happen later" and "They [Native Alaskans] leave without saying anything"); ABC books in translation; an untranslated tape of a storyteller; slides; clothes; and other artifacts. The way into first understanding, and the sharing of that exploration, seemed very comfortably to me to take this prose-poem format.

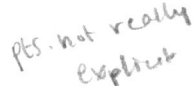

Writing to Note, Commemorate, Save, and Savor

I've been in teaching for forty-two of my forty-seven years—as student, teacher, student again, teacher again. Sure, there are some limitations to living within such walls, but it's also a life (and those years were woven together with other life experiences, from a first job working the candy counter at Woolworth's back when there still were Woolworth's to several travelogues that included hitch-hiking across the Sahara from Niger to Algeria). I don't like being told that I'm not really living, as in "living in the real world." Our worlds are what we make them and I'm astonished—as I try to show in this poem—by how slowly school lore and school assignments change, for schools are large cultures within our cultures, communities within our community. Important to us all.

I consider my son coming home to tell me the same new old joke or school legend I heard as a child. I remember my daughter coming home with the same assignment that I did as a fourth-grader, so I shouldn't be surprised when her brother follows suit three years later, different teacher, same school culture. And after all, shouldn't we celebrate some of that continuity even as we work for productive changes within it?

Here in the New World

I'm making Norwegian meatballs for the second
time in my life, for elementary school—4th grade's
write-about-your-cultural-heritage-week; this year

for my son, the youngest. I know now to make the meat-
balls smaller and cook them longer. Three years ago,
my daughter watched hawk-steady over spitting oil,

then made a face of adult-food dismay
when she tried her first. I've changed too
in these years (while fourth grade continued on

like an established dream—"write a one page report
on an interesting ancestor"). I've moved from
Viking-rage to Newfoundland peace, ex-husband fallen

away at last with the bitter dregs of our years' poor harvests.
Today, my children go through their paces—Shetland ponies
wickering their excitements into green coastal fogs.

Simmering in pure cream, this meal is totally incorrect—
I've bound pork with beef, with egg, potatoes, and bread—
calories enough to fuel a northern winter. The black dog

slumps before the hot stove, enjoying our fragrant day
   dreams.
Friends have returned to Florida for solstice. And soon we'll
   all
return, from eonic darkness, like a carefully hummed song,

the one I've spent years growing used to. I hear it when we
eat together—fish and fowl—sour and spice and sweet—pass
   each
plate and toss our stories into the bone-dish of the future.

Writing to Critique;
Writing to Poke Fun (Often at Oneself)

Where and how does school take place? As a class visitor—especially when observing new teachers of writing—I often learned more than I bargained for: The biggest lesson for this regular class observer who kept lists of T-shirt slogans, shoe types, ways to fidget or put on make-up in the slouched-low corner of the classroom, is how large students' lives are and how small we loom in them. Vivid memory: sitting six seats from the front of the writing classroom as the new young teacher launched her pedagogy boldly and loudly into all corners of the room and I watched the young woman in front of me snake her arm down to get *Hen in a Basket* crackers, one, another, another from the box hidden between her desk and mine, right in front of my toes, in fact. I couldn't help wondering at what moment she'd also crack open the can of Cheez-Whiz that sat on the floor by the box of crackers in order to make a more balanced meal out of the hour.

First-Year Writing—Florida

Spring touches first-year writing:
pink bicycle shorts, many large interlocking loop earrings,
gold, some silver, day's growth, no growth, polka dot
hairbows, midriff tops and salmon shirts, strong calves,
tender anklebones over no socks, light-longing, teacher-
dazed. Backpack footrest. Pen like a knife, balky log, shaft
of hope, pure task. Digital and analog. Citrus shirts, spiked
palm hair, hair like metal, hair like a lawn of hair, trimmed
into style. Khakis, deck tennis shoes above bikini socks
above steamy brown industrial carpet; coral nails tap,
knees shake, underground applause. Chains and charms
under collars, chains over collars with hanging coin, star,
shell, fish, cross. Tapping irregular binder paper straight.
Ticonderoga, rollerball, three-pocket folder. Luminous co-
balt shades, acne, tortoise shells, last row squints, voice of
egret, ibis, loon, broken surf, foghorn, reef. Cacophony's
scents—flower, stale, raw—flushed smiles, all-nighter eyes,
shredded shorts safety pinned closed, serious full bodied,
bend across desk, tap, tease a friend, ask a question again
again again. Lost, found, keys, umbrellas, thoughts, facts,
the right word, the perfect ending—
finesse the draft,
class of sighs,
sunset
sunrise,
start again?

The Cheez-Whiz, I have to admit, was never deployed. But I still recall my teacherly amazement at the woman's gall which made me take my own classroom seriousness in the future with a dollop of American processed spread. The poem "First-Year Writing" tries to walk the delicate line between two pedagogical versions—students' and teacher's—while finding both sides admirable in their hopefulness.

Writing to Highlight Contradictions

Parent as teacher, teacher as parent. There's no end to staggering literacy insights. Our children show us the inside of classrooms, our classrooms sometimes feel like rooms full of our children—who take us through the rainbow of relational emotions each day, week, year. It's a pedagogical potlatch, and well worth attending to.

Homework

he says, *is stupid.*
Seventy spelling words,
*that's fourteen words, times five
times each,* in cursive, and he
is left-handed. Letters
smear across his Superman
T-shirt. He dismantles
the disposable pencil. I ask
that he not pull the eraser
out with his teeth.
Because it can choke you
I say. He leers, bares pre-
molars, milky canines, curled
lips, an eight-year-old's show-me
disdain. *How?* You could
swallow it. An interesting
science problem, it seems;
he traces the trajectory with a finger
from Adam's apple, around Superman's
large red S in the red diamond,
filled in with mustard yellow.
I x-ray in, see a cartoon eraser
tumbling past his ribs
and vertebrae, wedging
into an important air passage,
despite my entreaties. *Fifteen left.*
Hedgehog small, he sneaks off,
watches TV, turned down
and up close, nearly uncurled,
feet on the screen. *Six more.*
He dances a little yogurt down
sneaks a moment's peace
in the dog's ruff, careens
outside into his evening orbit.
I need a break! Neighbor's basketball

on the driveway like a heartbeat
behind his clear high free
indifferent scream.

It is crucially common among writers that we learn by watching the struggles and triumphs of our own children. [your own memories]

Writing to Become a Better Reader, Writer, Teacher

I've come to know and value poetry as a life process, certainly a process involved in the making and contemplating of artistic texts, but an art that is also, and as importantly, a journey back to the unconscious, a relearning and realigning of selves. These are the ways I live poetry now and would teach it to others. I send friends new poems on e-mail, each for a separate reason: with one it's a diary of my life, as poems sometimes are for me; with one it's a signal of trust; with one I can preen and be proud as I'm not supposed to be in public: communication, sharing, pure pleasure.

As is no doubt true for many readers of this collection, much of my (academic) world is constructed on the internet these days.

I
send poems,
flirt,
create,
critique,
arrange childcare,
transmit data,
respond to students,
schedule,
converse,
obscure,
share too freely,
get stuffy and irritated,
flattened out,
affectless,
elated
don't answer,

> lose text,
> find text I didn't expect,
> invent a new world,
> a friendly English Department,
> a universe.

Yet many of my students have been floating through this textual ether longer and farther than I have. In that sense, it's their world. But I find value in sharing it. And in return, I can write and share poems about composing as I know it, as a senior learner eager to share the process:

How Does a Poem Start?

At the beginning of each picture there is someone who works with me. Toward the end I have the impression of having worked without a collaborator.
    —Christian Zervos—Conversation with Picasso
       in *The Creative Process*

I thought I saw you
over my left shoulder,
out the study window,
down the centipede grass lawn,
just brushed on the forehead
by the cabbage palm fronds.
As I counted out syllables
on my lips, I was sure your lips
moved. You waved, as I turned
a line, enjambed myself
into the evening.
For I can sit working
as long as the city sleeps
and stars float
like separate spyholes
in the sky's humidity.
Deciding there is a door
for each star,
I open each
to see what is really

just outside this picture.
And only after such euphoria,
do I notice that you are gone.

I've never been one to think that analyzing how I write demystifies it. If anything, it deepens and enriches the mystery while giving me encouragement and insight and some reason(s) to continue on.

Writing to Investigate, to Shed New Light on Issues

Within the following poem, I store a particular memory (I can remember composing it, sitting in my back workroom, feeling like I could hear my daughter growing older in the evening darkened house for I could, literally, hear her breathing); the poem was also written to have a text to share the next day with my poetry group, and to explore a form—quatrains—I would be teaching that week to my poetry students, and includes thematically recurrent motifs for me. I was reading; I had been doing a lot of writing about writing and remembering old travels. Before children I traveled a lot and now I saw I was traveling through them. Vaulted into my own future by my daughter's aging, actual life felt dream-like, causing me to remember one of my own recurrent (and I knew common enough) dreams, that of floating over a city. All these flashforwards and flashbacks combined into one interwoven meditation; what I call the process of writing a poem.

Night Songs

My daughter sings herself older in her bedroom
before sleeping. This is the sound of her self-flute:
tones float through a darkened house, loose
lean counterpoint to my evening's journey.

Sleep-awake myself, I leaf through anthologies,
throw I-Chings of poetry. Craft can frame
old messages a new way, blow longings secretly
into bottles: they drift along the inland waterways

of personal history. Enough densely scored songs,
enough possibility, and she falls to dreams. I have
that one we all have: float high above the city—not waving
not worried—assume I've finally pinched myself awake.

On the first day of writing classes, though, if I'm not careful, I *won't* talk about the way the poetry group helps each member re-finding and re-defining through words; how friends use poems for understanding their teaching, how I use poems about daughters to talk to my daughter (as well as to the daughter I was to my mother and to other writers who mother poems), how writing is meditation and rehearsal for my friend Devan as she walks around Lake Ella and then later shares that insight with me on e-mail, part of our poetry conversation.

If I'm not careful, the-profession-and-the-teacher-over-my-shoulder will whisper that I should not talk about Lake Ella and poetry writing, that I should only emphasize craft, solitude and aesthetic distance. And there's a reason for this impulse; it was how I was taught. So I can use my writing to investigate my own literacy. How I was taught is so much part of how I teach that it deserves my creative attention.

Writing to Theorize and Investigate Positions; Writing to Argue and Persuade

One of my most basic theories about teaching is that many of us come to our profession from similar but opposing impulses. We hope to right the wrongs of a teaching past, the kind of past I investigate here.

> **Workshop Memory**
> In my first-year graduate workshops, young men and women sit in a half-circle around a famous white-haired poet. He smokes a pipe, pages through our work, drops matches, and doesn't intervene during our remarks to each other. No comments beyond the significant twitch of an eyebrow or speedy movement to the next text.

I thumb the *Norton Anthology of Modern Poetry* to figure out what poets write about. I am embarrassed by the women—Sylvia and her anger and Anne and her body. I mention loudly that I never want to be called a woman poet. I never mention that I have bought all of Anne Sexton's books and read them, yet rarely buy the assigned others: Wordsworth floated outside my experience—a young man's life, what was that to me? I say none of this in class, although I write a lot. Although I didn't know I couldn't be a poet, I did know I felt terrible when it came to my voice. I stumbled if I read aloud. Attending poetry readings, I'd see real poets: How could I impress in the manner of William Everson, Robert Bly or Gary Snyder, low, vibrant voices seducing audiences with words? As a fellowship student at a summer writer's conference, I was momentarily mentored. The poet reviewing my manuscript suggested that I not use the name "Wendy" to publish under. I obeyed him, using W.S. Bishop for five years in my insecurity. And during that time, I wrote about my family. My young loves. A chapbook compiled for me by a willing small-press editor seemed to be composed primarily of those of my poems that had the word *thigh* in them.

During those same years, I drew upon few resources and began to teach writing myself.

Or we teach to return the investment others made in us: we teach because we were drawn to the profession by the passions of other teachers we admire. Well, that's one theory and as with most theories, the answer may lie somewhere in the territory of both/and. Story and memory certainly help me explore my pedagogical beliefs as do research and primary and secondary research. Not either/or but both/and. "Othering" could be read as an attempt to understand those who think that teaching is "not real life" by imagining other lives. It could be read as one of my attempts to understand students (or teachers or theorists or writers) who hold dear beliefs that are far different from those I hold. In addition, it argues for the power of imagination—a power you see deployed again and again by the authors in this collection.

Introduction

Othering

Once, I tried to imagine it—

not reading—nothing—not clouds, nor the inky residue
of night; not the pages of sheets rumpled at bedside;
not squirrels chattering on weathered fences,
responding to the inquisitions of winter; not
typescripts of age, skin of children tightening
into more serious play; not summer sun hurling out flames
until the day's hammocks melt into their seasonal plots;
not ever to enjoy the novelties of spring;

not sleeping—no singular cocoon of escape
while oceans and winds beat the planet out of perfect orbit;
no swimming deeper to grasp air bubbles of hope
and ride them to the surface; no clasp of sweaty terror
redeemed by daylight; never to enter the broadest texts
of stillness, to recount genealogies into darkness;
no begats or regrets; no blinding luck, no tomb, cave,
diurnal stone-tumbled renewal; no luck;

not eating—never coming sweetsour to one's senses
playing across the tongue; no luncheons on lawns
under canopy trees; no Italian terraces and cheese rinds
of nostril-fluting delicacy; no seeking, no Braille
of spice and salt, ocean-scent of body's luck; no reason
to stroke the belly, flat or convex; simply existing within
the absence of—; no tides of flesh, green howls
of unrooting; no blame, no satiety, no animal ease;

not loving—fingers rude and blunt—mere digits, bland
instruments; not waiting or wanting; no breath of moon
in the ear of dawn; solitary and unaware of absence,
or absent and not missed; featherless, wings furled;
untouched by cataclysm; earthbound on an empty road; no
   attitude
toward sunset; chorus of frogs lost on infinite jetstreams
where blue sky reclines, a lonely god; not made in anyone's
   image—
literate, impervious, dull; and rarely, if ever, heard from;

if other, so little then to make of life, of this, of life, this—this.

Through the generous sharing of the contributors to this collection, I've learned I don't have to praise pedagogy—another part of "this—this"—quietly, furtively, belligerently, or apologetically. The work gathered here makes my arguments for me, showing us how we should and can celebrate our lives in literacy. I'm reminded, in fact, of the way Robert Hass begins his poetry collection *Praise*. At the start of his collection he places a Mellville-esque epigraph in which a "captain" is asked how he will deal with his encounter with an immense beast "terrifying, and unpredictable." The captain thinks a minute and then says: "I think I shall praise it" (Hass 1).

Useful advice for engaging this unpredictable beast we call teaching.

Works Cited

Bishop, Wendy. *Released into Language: Options for Teaching Creative Writing*. 2nd ed. Portland, ME: Calendar Islands P, 1998.

———. *Teaching Lives: Essays and Stories*. Logan, UT: Utah State UP, 1997.

Hass, Robert. *Praise*. NY: Echo, 1979.

Part One

From and For Classrooms

First Night of Class

LAURA APOL

Nothing begins with us—
not this story or any other.

Andromeda does not slow her dizzying spin
nor does a field of wheat
wait. We catch our plane

mid-flight; below us, time
fades like a prim border of pines
while the sky opens wide as
god's blue eye.

We have far to go, navigating
between stars that appear only
after dark. The secret names

we were given at birth are cradled
in our curved hands.

It is a magic

world now, and we are at
the center, our own lives the map,

our words the edge of a knife
we are just beginning to hone.

The Poet Meets His Class in the Chemistry Lab

KEN AUTREY

The periodic chart is God here,
benign beginnings of everything
above the white-scrawled
blackboard, gas nozzles,
fierce arcing faucets,
acid-stained sinks.

The place dazzles with glass—
beakers, tubes, flasks,
and pipettes. Their very names
exude sulphurous fumes.
"Don't break anything,"
the poet says and bangs his briefcase
on the black lab table.

"Nothing's sacred here.
Alchemy lives," he proclaims
and fires up a bunson burner,
pulling cork-stoppered jars
from the shelves.
Apprentices fidget
on wooden stools. He mutters,
"Let's cook some poems."

Students push books aside
in the spirit of science.
They mix white powders
and golden liquids like so many
metaphors, improvising rhythms
in the spit and pop of the moment.
They are cast into their mothers'
kitchens again to concoct sauces
and dare each other to taste them.

tuesday 8:45

Joseph H. Ball

kirsten,
i had forgotten
when we planned
to discuss your
essay on john
cheever whose novels
touch on the bizarre
that yet another

meeting time and place arranged
                                by others
                                        of influence and power
over me and you

was scheduled   your paper
was quite interesting and   i was intrigued
by this transition

"in both novels there was
a specific homosexual experience"

thank you for that
a general homosexual experience is beyond
my imagination
        can we re-schedule for friday?

The English Teacher's Bad Day

GRACE BAUER

*Something there is
that doesn't love a wall*
I repeat as if they cared.

What do farmers hauling
rocks have to do
with their bodies still
tanned from Palm Beach
and Bermuda, their eighteen
year old's certainty of never
running out of life?

Last week when I warned them
more than one Willy Loman
might be sitting in
this very room, they exchanged
weary looks and rolled
their eyes, convinced
it must be me.

And who am I to say
they're wrong?
I, who force them
to define the elements of tragedy
in two-hundred-fifty words.

Teaching Poetry: A Way to Grace the World?

Kelly Cherry

Ever since someone suggested to me that teaching poetry may be a manifestation or exemplum of grace—something divine or deistic about it, though perhaps in the manner of a minor goddess, or a small, sacred spring (freely flowing, inclined to bubble)—I have been trying to figure out how I might put the idea of grace together with the idea of academia. I teach at the University of Wisconsin in Madison. UW is a huge bureaucracy, and surely nobody ever got "bureaucracy" and "grace" into the same sentence. It's true that in my time at UW I've known a dean or two who plainly thought he ought to be addressed as "Your Grace," but presumably that's not exactly what my acquaintance had in mind.

Do I feel graceful or gracious when I teach? No. I usually feel like I should have had a second cup of coffee before I came to class. Do I feel I'm a conduit for poetry's saving grace, a kind of priest conferring poetic blessings upon my students? I wish!

In spite of their early-morning grogginess, in spite of—if they are budding writers or scholars—their egos, and—if we are in the Humanities Building—in spite of the lack of even one window, my students do sometimes receive a blessing of poetry, a bloom of benediction showing in their flushed, surprised, and pleased faces, but the poems do that, not I.

The legend of the Humanities Building, by the way, is that it is as ugly as it is because the contractor misread the blueprints and built it wrong side out. They say that the architect, upon seeing the result, hanged himself. This is easy to believe, because it's what we all feel we want to do after several hours in a room with no window and with fluorescent lights buzzing a lot worse than any fly Emily Dickinson ever heard.

Of course it is the students, each of them, whose presence alchemizes pedagogy into grace, so that the hapless professor, meaning me, you understand, can see a poem or the world in a new, lighted way, receive a vision of the possible. Maria, writing poems that practically ooze an enviable sensuality and playfulness, intense Meg, always achingly anxious and therefore ever precise and powerful in her lyrics, or brilliant—that says it all—Erin brings me a piece of shaped language that lifts me out of my frowning or scowling or, anyway, insufficiently caffeinated self. In my lit class, a student, a sorority pledge with long, lazy limbs that she stretches unself-consciously, says, "My college life up to now has been about drinking and socializing, and my friends thought I was crazy to sign up for this, but you know what? I'm discovering that I love reading poetry! And I'm beginning to believe I'm *good* at reading poetry!"

Now *that's* a benediction. That's when my face starts to flush, as I am surprised by joy.

Before Everything

DEVAN COOK

6:50 A.M., before everything
except coffee and newspaper—
before breakfast, dear students,
I sit down at my computer, send
my thoughts to you. Poetic? In truth
my oatmeal's cooling; timing
is crucial in oatmeal as in everything—
the everything I'm writing before—
and this poem is filler, before
oatmeal which is more filler.

By dawn—birds cry outside,
sunrise is soon—I will self-censor,
unsure whether to write or say
what I'm saying now: if I confused
or scared you yesterday, I'm sorry.
All those words required, so *much*
writing. I watch you reading
the list of course requirements,
but I can't read you.

Writing for my class is easy,
not as much work as it sounds
that first day. The syllabus
doesn't—can't—
say what's hard—
thinking, gaps, accidents,
finding places like this one
I've found now to fit
writing.
You have to make the place
to put the writing in;
you have to make the place
by writing.

The sun is up now, light
behind leaves, safe to go out—
time to walk my dog, run, not study.
Timing is everything,
wording your own time.
Fill it.

Wow – everyone should write their own this. (copy for now?)

Freshman Lit & Comp

STEPHEN COREY

>   for Janet Burroway

Wednesday evenings rooted to his place
—back row, nearest the door—
he had that plodding obstinance
of dullness laced with purpose.
Past twenty-five, pimpled and flabby,
bursting out of himself
at every tuck and button.
Arriving and leaving alone.

Never an answer, never a question,
hauling himself toward me every week
from the wood lathe of his job
in a low-grade furniture shop,
ready for commas, Milton, paragraphs, Donne.
Every other week, another essay
into listlessness and error,
as if the writing meant no more
than the grease he carried on his cuffs.

The *Iliad* provided the finish.
Six years later, I still can paint
the slants and tones of sunlight
mapped across my desk, or sing
the fossils deep below me
in those moments when I read
his final thesis of our course:

>   That the truest choice by Homer
>   was the crippling of Hephaestus,
>   for only the damaged could understand
>   the shield scrolled with gentle iron lace,
>   the aura that holds around the perfect forging.

english 098

PHEBE DAVIDSON

look at her
stone glass-eye bitch
"Write!"
she says
and hands out paper
just as if we wanted it
"Write!" she says
as if we had nothing
better to do with our lives
than put marks on paper
and act like
we like
it

when she looks
at us
what does she see—
does she see us?
does she see me?
yellow face, brown face
white face too
wanting to chew her up
and spit her out
instead of just
paper and
words

Childbearing Hips

ALLISON JOSEPH

Around the workshop table in this advanced
undergraduate class, my students tussle
over this one phrase, the women grimacing,
complaining, the men baffled as to why these
two words have sparked this protracted fight over

what to them is a love poem, a gentle
one at that. The men lean back in their chairs, fold
their arms across their chests, or worse, roll their eyes,
exasperated by offended females.
The women claim the phrase is just another

way to say fat, that it's anything but sweet,
and I can guess that memories of every
secret body shame are coursing through their minds,
ill-fitting training bras, rolls of belly fat,
hips grown too wide to wear that one pair of jeans

that fit all through high school. *You could just say "hips"*
one woman suggests, *childbearing makes her sound like
a cow,* while the author starts to protest,
then falls silent, succumbing to workshop's rule:
no talking about your poem while the class

talks about your poem. Two little words and
one huge rift he can't explain, at least until
I say he can. One man shouts, *what's wrong with child-
bearing hips? Isn't that why women were made?*
The women stiffen further, *typical male*

and *is that all we're good for* rising from their lips
quicker than I can stammer *let's look at the
poem's form* or *are lines two and three clichés?*
All the women care about is beauty, not

reproduction, so I delay revealing

that the phrase makes me cringe—visions of body
parts gone flabby going through my mind. At this
impasse, all I can do is stop the class, let
the author speak, but nothing he can say will
appease the angry faces glaring at him,

their bodies one subject they prefer his words
not touch, no apologies permitted here.

Workshop Pantoum

ALLISON JOSEPH

Does anybody want to start this off?
I think the second line has got to go.
Then silence, shuffled papers, a cough.
This poem tells too much, it doesn't show.

I think the second line has got to go.
The poem's author fidgets in his seat.
This poem tells too much, it doesn't show,
but still I thought it had a rhythmic beat.

The poem's author fidgets in his seat,
chews on a pencil, runs fingers through his hair.
But though I thought it had a rhythmic beat,
I didn't like its message of despair.

Chewing on a pencil, fingers through his hair,
the poet wants to tell us what we've missed.
I didn't like its message of despair—
the poems I prefer express life's bliss.

The poet wants to tell us what we've missed,
and when discussion's done, he lets us know
the poems he prefers express the bliss
of being all alone, friendless, with no

discussions intended to let him know
how he should write. Silence, another cough.
He broods, alone. *Anything more? No?*
Ok, next. Anybody want to start this off?

Open Letter to My Students

Kathleen Kirk

Here's the difference between us:
I don't know what a hackey sack is
but I looked for it
in the *American Heritage*
and the *Webster's Collegiate*.

It wasn't there.

So I asked you, and you laughed,
but I got an answer.
Only you can tell me the names
of the things in your world.

"We don't really care," you say,
"about your world."
Well, I do. I care
what it's made of,

whether it's glued or sewn,
what it's got inside,
what you do with it—
whether you kick it or toss it—

and how it's really spelled.

I care about the letter you sent
and the day your mother moved away,
about the miscarried child,
and the woman you love.

I care about how the moon
rose in your window
and how it watched over the park
with its hidden flowers.

Open Letter to My Students

I care about the dream you had,
the boy you lost,
the way someone left you
closed in a shell.

I'm not sentimental:
I don't ache or rage or pine
if I think you're overacting
but now I can name
the things of your world:

the keys,
the jar,
the wire scraped along concrete,
the balcony,
the hackey sack.

Taking the World Literature Class Outside

JANET McCANN

you, propped on the liveoak
drifting toward sleep
& watching the spider spin—
yes, even our writer's
name is soporific,

dostoyevski, say it
again & again, the wind
faint in the leaves,
dostoyevski, & if

Myshkin himself should
step from behind the trees
clothed in symbolic light,
would you wake up then?

braided girl dressed
in the letters LOVE,
lounging at my feet,
you say you would not
be false like Aglaya
but then, people are
nicer now,

& you with the short
hair & button-down
collar, you tell me
socialists are intolerable,
even in literature,
and clearly Dostoyevski
was one,

but no one is listening,
you are not even listening

Taking the World Literature Class Outside

& the shadows sharpen
as the sun moves from behind
a cloud. a far church

rings three chimes
& we are scattered by
two joyous Labradors!

Literacy:
Or How I Ended Up at the Old Folks Home

ANNE-MARIE OOMEN

In my battered Kalkaska classroom,
the old man had come, asking
help with his letters.

Don't need much.
Just enough reading to get through these
out loud. He held out

a dozen frayed children's books,
running his hands over the covers
like they were fine cloth.

He was eighty and bent,
and his candle eyes scared me some.
Told me he'd been a military man,

Never had to read long as I didn't get too high up.
Could always command a rank private
to read something for me—kid would think it was a test.

I assumed grandchildren
somewhere in the picture,
that's why the kiddy books.

Letters by heart the first week,
then mouthing short words in order. No speed,
but what he wanted, he wanted hard.

The day of the snowstorm,
he walked through drifts four feet high
to my house for a private lesson.

Literacy: Or How I Ended Up at the Old Folks Home

Don't have much time to do this,
got to keep at it.
Once, sounding out in class, he stumbled.

(Diphthongs, those odd blurrings
are murder for older readers.)
He cursed and left the room.

I'll lose my chance,
he muttered all down the hall,
head lowered like a boy's.

Out here in the snowbelt,
there are moments a person gets pushed too far.
Winter comes on hard.

Once, he came in rivered with tears.
Picture books ain't enough,
he shouted at me.

She's got to have the words.
Give me the words.
I led him into the long hallway.

Who is she? Outside
the steamy window, freezing rain.
Milwyn, my wife.

He stared down the hall,
all the way to the end. Ticking
ice on the glass.

He rubbed his hands up and down his sleeves,
and would not look at me.
You better tell me, Henry.

Long pauses ribbed with breathing,
She's got the mind disease, that Alzheimer's,
only thing she listens to anymore

*is those kiddies' books, and only if they
got words. She sits by me then,
and somedays, she'll still hold my hand.*

*I don't know how it works, but she's got
to have the words, won't listen anymore
unless there are words on the page.*

*You got to help me, girl,
you got to make me know the words.*
And so I sit near them

and cue him with the hard ones,
pitch fork, whalesong, frittering,
all the way through, story after story,

watching her cuddle under his arm,
watching the old way of love, his
gallantry, her coyness,

watching language unlock a marriage,
how words open thought up and out,
spreading like bright wings over their faces.

Watching My Students Write
Robert Parham

This is why I am here: to watch them work.

They think, even my bosses believe, I teach,
but the truth is as obvious as their scrawls.

I am that proverbial guide we pretend to be,
the one who leads them into the ripe jungle
of the mind and shows them the fruit and nuts,
even offers up the names and kinds. I smile
and leave, like some fraternity joker spent
by impractical jests. I look over my shoulder
and say "Harvest them, eat what is to be eaten,
save the seeds of what is worthy or practical
or beautiful: separate, consume, save, enjoy."

They are at first confused, but appetite
and desperation take over eventually.

One boy takes out his Barlow and slices a gold
and green fruit. A girl asks what it is. It smells,
he says, and pulls back his head. Too rich,
he tosses it aside, but another boy picks it up,
pushes at its heart with his only tool at hand,
his finger, and dislodges a piece. He likes
its color, its feel. He nibbles at it, smiles,
and offers to share it. A serious sort, he
is trusted, and others join in. A girl has cracked
a nut the size of a melon. Inside are ants
and maggots. She frowns, drops it to the side,
where a football player edges away from old
things again. They make a territory, defeat
hunger and discover that curiosity
is a paradox, for in feeding it, one
makes it an appetite, the kindest of all.

Flattened by Flattery

TERRY RASMUSSEN

he catches me off guard
his large sleepy brown eyes set
in such a perfectly beautiful face
he enters my office smiling shyly
one arm behind his back
to present a bouquet of cream and mauve-colored mums
his voice warm and flirtatious
because you're my favorite teacher
yours the only class worth getting out of bed
my heart, my head rise and swell
my cheeks begin to burn
until I remind myself
of my classroom identity, my position
he's majoring in medicine, not English
he's the age of my own son
but
his face is so sincere
the flowers so lovely

he catches me off guard again
when he asks to make up last week's exam
foolish woman, I chide myself
foolish, silly old woman

Nervouswork

WILLIAM SNYDER, JR.

Saturday morning, and orange juice and the heater's buzz,
and outside, the first Alberta Clipper—snow-spray
blusters past the window. A brain surgeon on the radio—
and I hear the tears in his voice—says
how good he feels sometimes repairing spines. He does
more spines than brains, he says, and with both, no room
for mistake. And there lies the satisfaction. Sure.

Like in class yesterday, the reticence, the silence—
just one of those days, or Friday, or too few
had read too little. Whatever. But, silence. So I refused
to speak—puttered through my notes, underlined
more lines, watched them fidget, shuffle feet, roll
eyes. And so I waited. Until, on the cusp of a riot, Jordi
couldn't stand it and got things going—she scores
for the soccer team—said she'd read
her in-class piece, her discussion on love. Someone you love
will always be there for you, no matter what, she read,
and she asked Gabe to read. And with a grimace, and a breath
he did: You would die for the person you truly loved—
and it was around our circle, Gabe asking Katy, Katy
asking Anne, Mike, Rhianna reading meanings of love,
just what love is. And they all felt good, buoyed
by share, control. By love. But I am professor, and so
I suggested omission—they were, it seemed, thinking ideal,
ignoring the real, real love in the day-to-day.
Silence then. And shoulders sagged, eyes fell. Silence.

Morning drifts toward lunch, *Cartalk* on in a bit. Three crows
wrestle gusts on the backyard fence. And I think,
that though I could not begin to slice muscle
around a spine, that I too work in a world of brain, and of
heart to boot, and what may be a blessing is this:
my mistakes are not so calamitous as that surgeon's might be,
but my regrets must be every bit as fine. Every bit.

Preciousness of Imperfection

WILLIAM SNYDER, JR.

I'm getting so frustrated, she says, this is so
confusing. Angela sits in the student chair
in button-down blue shirt, white sweater-shirt
beneath, jeans—front of one cuff flipped up
exposing oval of sock. Could she
not have noticed? The computer hums.
Students chatter down the hall. We consider topics
for the argument essay, small topics
from the heart, from experience. What about
bilingual education? she asks. That will need
research, I say. I'm so frustrated, she says, and I hate
to choose a simple topic, you know, like abortion
or euthanasia, ones everybody does. Maybe like,
I'm just saying, I like the little topics, you know,
like that one in class: you shouldn't tell white lies.
Yes, I say, I like that one too.

I'm the kind of person, she says, who likes to be
challenged. I know, I say. What about
stay-at-home-dads? she asks. I'm skeptical, I say.
Like, that they shouldn't be ostracized.
That there is nothing really truly womanish about
working in the house, nothing that says just women
can do those things. I think you have something, I say.

Brown shoes, knobby soles. Eyes that see you
when she speaks. This young woman, Angela,
sits by my desk, and as we talk, figure, plan—
that cuff. Curled in the dryer perhaps, creased
in the folding, or at some small moment
of thinking or dream she scratched her shin, forgot
to flip it back. I fall in love with this odd cuff,
the white-ribbed sock, with Angela too—her trial
of choosing. And with those kids in the hall.
And with me even. With all of us, gone as we are
to confusion and flaw.

There Are Miracles Extant In This World

WILLIAM SNYDER, JR.

At the premier of Haydn's 96th, a chandelier
fell from the ceiling. Luckily, no one was hurt.
Since then, it's been called the Miracle. I, too,
remember when the roof caved in. My students
protesting the journal assignment. So much
bullshit, they said. Or later, my pickiness
with lates. Like, time is relative, they said,
what's a minute? Chill out. Or when they grumbled
that writing is too personal—it comes
from the heart. It shouldn't be changed. On and on.
But it's how I do it, I said.
And it could've been worse: the chandelier
could've struck a cello, or a cello player, or a
patron who loved the cello, or I could've
required those five paragraph themes.
Now, I bubble in my grades—mostly A's and B's

The Portuguese Princess Looks to the East

THOMAS STEIN

The Portuguese Princess looks to the east
from my cubicle at the university remediation center
formerly the fine arts dept painting and sculpture studio.

When I was hired as "writing specialist for at risk students"
the Princess was leaning between some filing cabinets
with other Zoe Beiler canvasses—Beiler taught painting in the
    thirties.

While confessing partiality to a sullenly fezed Turk
conscientiously wiping blood from the blade of his scimitar
I hesitated hanging Beiler's conventional oils above

my desk in the writing skills cubicle
but eventually placed the Princess in prominence
between Beiler Homestead and Badlands Landscape.

The eyes of the Princess are dark impassive alert &
placidly ignore the onlooker.
Olive cheeks rouged lips expressively closed

tight black curls spill out from beneath bright headscarves
down over a shawl peasant blouse & skirt in a palette
that testifies to Beiler's struggle with Cezanne.

The Princess seduces—how pleasant
standing at your easel afternoon sun
falling through floor to ceiling windows

painting portraits of friends & classmates
disguised in exotic garb of royalty & headsmen
when trains still ran no

The Portuguese Princess Looks to the East

oil booms busted retention concerned or
wire fence abstracted antelope prairie.
The Portuguese Princess looks to the east

from my remediation center writing cubicle
while warm afternoon winds insist we look westward
to an early evening that may or may not be.

The Big Up

LARRY STRAUSS

That first month no one would do my homework. Instead, I'd get drawings, torn-out magazine pages, notes that had been passed around the back row of desks, or blank sheets of wide rule. I blamed it on the effect of television. That passive medium had lulled them all into an intellectual stupor. Everything my students knew seemed to come from the streets of their neighborhood or from the electronic myth factory. I lectured students on how the mass media was brainwashing them and made that the topic of their next essay, due Friday.

"It's a stupid assignment," said Edgar Martinez, after the bell rang.

"Do you watch TV?" I asked him.

"Yeah," said Marco, his homeboy.

"Do you believe everything you see on it?"

"Not really." Marco was the taller of the two. His ears curled away from his shaved head.

"Write down some of the things you don't believe."

Their smiles suggested I wasn't the first rookie who thought he could turn them into real students.

"Don't you want to graduate? Do something with your lives?"

"We up already," Edgar said.

"Up?" I wondered, aloud.

"Fox Undercover," Marco added. "Tonight at ten. You got a TV set? You could come over my house..."

I don't know how Edgar and Marco were chosen to represent the taggers of Los Angeles but that night at 10:25 on Channel Eleven I saw my two students spray-painting a freeway sign and various interior and exterior walls. Standing in front of their freshly scrawled names, they were asked, by someone behind the camera, why they did it?

"To be *up*," Marco said.

Edgar added: "To be famous."

In class the next day I told them that they ought to spend their free time on homework rather than defacing public property.

"I did your *pinché* homework," Marco said, and reached into his back pocket for a slice of neatly folded paper covered with one long paragraph in the same angular print as his graffiti.

"Yeah, me too," Edgar said. His was written on the back of a flyer for a $9.95 per month pager service.

"Weren't you busy watching yourselves on TV?" I asked.

"That's right," Edgar said. "We up now—the *big* up!"

"Don't wanna look stupid," Marco added. "So hurry up and teach us something."

Edgar and Marco did become better students, though it may have been too late. That spring Marco's father was crushed by falling debris at the construction site where he worked. Marco got a full-time job to help support his family. The last time I saw him he was painting houses with an uncle. Edgar stayed in school but couldn't put together enough credits to graduate. I wonder if Edgar and Marco remember their moment in the spotlight—or if they've managed to find recognition, another big up, in some other way. Their names in my story might have done it—except that out of respect for their privacy I've changed them.

Logical Fallacies

ALISON TOWNSEND

(during the Gulf War)

This morning I taught my Freshman English class
how to avoid logical fallacies. *Post hoc,*
ergo propter hoc, ad hominem, non sequitur.
"Simple errors in thinking," I said,
"can lead to something demonstrably wrong
in your conclusion."

I wrote examples I'd memorized on the board
as if I believed them, teaching my students
how to fortify their arguments
with reasoning packed as tightly as sandbags
that can hold back a river, altering floodwaters
and redirecting their flow.

"Make your writing bulletproof," I said,
the inside of my head a curtain of blowing sand,
grit working its way in through the tent flaps,
the grains sharp-edged, each one an irritant
layered with the potential of pearl.

But how do we hold sand in the sea of the body?

Halfway through, I wanted to say it was all wrong,
that every example I'd provided was false,
as unconnected to real life
as the textbook we held in our hands.

What's interesting is the light
filtering in between the floorboards
of each quivering sentence, uneven and beautiful
as the foundations of old houses
that shift and sigh with the land,

settling into themselves
the way a bird turns in its nest
or a child leans into her mother,
making a home in the shape of her body,
driven by deeper rules
than the logic we unroll around us
like bales of barbed wire,
believing ourselves lucky or safe.

All the snowy owl has to do
is open her white wings to persuade us,
a prayer of feathers outlined
against the winter sky.

Perspective

PATRICIA VALDATA

In the overheated classroom
Twenty students lean back,
Feet on empty chairs. They wear an odd

Mix of winter and summer clothes,
As the shrubs and trees outside show
Faded red berries, swelling red buds.

Through the open rear window,
The class seems to extend to Delaware
Avenue, along the brick path

Whose fence posts connected by arcs of
Heavy chain compress into a black line,
Flanked on one side by old brick dorms,

On the other, dying elms. There on the lawn
A black Labrador waves its tail like a
Banner and leaps to catch a frisbee, where

Once a red-tailed hawk caught a squirrel
And stood, talon-deep in fur, tearing the
Flesh with its beak as students passed by.

Stone Dreams

Jane Elkington Wohl

with the Central Middle School Sixth Grade

When I first went to his house I could not understand
why Dainis had placed a stone on top of each fence post,
as if, here in the Wyoming mountains, the wind
might suddenly uproot them all and whip
great lines of fence into the sky, rusted barbed wire tails
of some weathered wooden kite but then
he told me about his dream of the great stone opening
like a mouth, like Jonah's whale, taking him in
until, in this dream, rock filled with light
and all the people stood, washed with it.

Today I asked the children to tell me
stone dreams. Look, I said, look at the stone
I have placed on your desk, what does it dream, does it
dream at all, does it dream about the streaks of color,
the veins of green or red along its sides, does it dream of
the boulder it once was part of?
What would you dream if you were this stone,
what would you dream about this stone?
I read them a poem by another teacher who asks the same
     question
and whose students tell him "stones don't dream."

I draw circles on the board...see, I say, the way he
remembers stones and students, remembers childhood chestnuts
gathered like shiny stones, filling the bag until
it breaks and he sits on the ground holding the
burnished solid spheres
and remembers again?
What does the stone remember?

The thin blond girl writes "My dreams are like stones, strong, and round.
I treasure them, like stones in colored boxes."
Another child writes "I am a little person, I walk into
rooms filled with crystal chips inside the stone" and I remember
Dainis' dream and the light-filled rock. "I am a little person
and I walk inside the stone"
and then
the small tense boy with glasses writes
five lines, tears the notebook paper small,
small enough to fit the little poem
about a stone underground, in the dark, under
the earth, ground pressing down
then suddenly the stone is
"dreaming of a flower."

The room stills,
dark smell of loam and earth falls
at our feet while brilliant dahlias bloom, and imagined
color flares against the dreaming stone,
orange lilies and Christmas amaryllis.
What do you think? I ask the class
"I think," Stephanie says, "it's about
sometimes we think we know a person
and we really don't."

Teaching Reading

JANE ELKINGTON WOHL

Ginger root gnarls in my hand
above the cilantro, parsley, eggplant
dark as midnight
dust clings to my fingers.
Change slips and jingles in the check-out line.

Ellen hated herself so much that when
I, as her teacher, asked her to do math,
she bit her hand and retreated
to the nest of blankets in the corner,
curling her bird-bone legs and arms
up tight against her. We might forget
that she was there.

One day she asked to learn to read,
eleven years old, but time meant nothing.
In rivers some water continues swirling, caught
in a back wash, an eddy, a violent pool
behind a rock.
"Teach me to read," she asked.

I slice onion, sauté, stir,
add ginger, garlic,
the kitchen fills with smells
red and green peppers, chicken.

What do I learn from this?

I will not touch a candle flame.
Tea leaves hold no secrets for me.

Ellen's thin neck curves above her desk.
She learns the story of the princess she wants to be.
She will not take the pages home but asks
me to keep them for her in my teacher's desk.

There is no happy ending here.

Day by day she works,
builds sentences with word cards,
long white lines across the classroom floor.
She learns not to bite herself.
Her mother dies.

I boil rice and set the table.

One day at recess in the small school yard,
she stayed close to my side, repeating,
"Hold my hand, Jane, hold my hand, please,
so I don't get lost." As if the smallest human touch could
save her.

I have created an imaginary meal.
What nourishment does writing bring?

In the face of bravery, we must fall back,
decode those marks on paper.
Once again, she steps out across the ice.

On the last day of school, late June,
the Philadelphia magnolias gone, the air humid
thick, the buses wait. She turns, stops,
"See you tomorrow, Jane," she says,
"See you tomorrow."
She climbs on finally
and the bus drives off.

how sad!

PART TWO

Language and the World

Ask Nick, Heather, Dave to send to parents Don's heartfelt peace

The Dream of Teaching

KEN AUTREY

Each fall I know the dream will come.
The room gapes cavernous, bleak,
layered with September light.
The chalkboard is scrubbed,
floor freshly oiled.
I stand in front of the class,
tie much too tight. My hands
grip the desk as if I'm straining
to lift it—or vault up
in a handstand. My change,
knife, keys, and pocketwatch
would clatter and bounce
on the bare desk.
The room has no geography;
I am locked in place.
If only I could see my hands,
utter one welcoming word, the faces
of my students would emerge,
books reappear and bloom again.

The Scholar

GRACE BAUER

deconstructs desire, confines
it in language, which is,
he says, its element, the source
from which it flows.

On some level, I suppose
he's right, but my mind
wearies from racing
to follow his train

of thought, and collides
head-on with memory
in a tunnel called love
in a landscape called pleasure

and silence is the only
comment I can make fit
you inside me and breathless
in a darkness for which
there are no words to signify.

Intro to Poetry

STEVEN BAUER

You thought it was math that taught
the relation of time and speed,
but it's farther than you knew
from that sun-lit white-walled classroom
to this darkened lounge with its couch
and overstuffed chairs. How many miles,
would you say, since we talked
as if poetry were no distorting mirror,

one-way street? But listen: sometimes
it's like this, a stranger's Ford pulls up
and you, with no plans for the afternoon,
get in. He doesn't talk, stares at the road
and it's miles before you understand
you didn't want to travel. His lips say *no*
as you reach for the radio's knob.

In this silence, you fall deeper
into yourself, and even the car
disappears, the stranger's face blurs
into faded upholstery, and all things
being equal, you're alone as though
you've wandered into a forest with night
coming on, no stars, the memory of sun
and a voice asking, *Is this my life?*

The Death of Reading

DARRELL FIKE

Damn the inventor of the highlighter pen
that smug tool that effaces without eradicating
that shreds a text without leaving a scar,
a pastel weapon of destruction
suspended above the page like a tiny guillotine blade.

Windshield Vipers (Keeping Time)

KATHERINE M. FISCHER

careening through snowy
hillsides, the evergreens
dappled with ice, late
winter morning melting
into violets
right before our very
noses, my colleague
and I travel to the conference.
his nostrils flaring in the air
to the rhythm of wind
shield wipers, he
drones on dripping
syllables of "poststructural-
positionedness"
and "monolithic religiosity" in
vampire literature. he bites
text in two, sinking fangs
of academe into
passion's neck
while I steer
and crank
down the window
to catch the faint
small sweetness
of pooling
sap.

Wrestle Theory

ALICE GEORGE

If a) either there are no truly interesting 'ideas' or b) language can't carry them across the river anyway, then c) whenever we have an idea we should keep it away from language, we should tie a rope around its neck and let it howl in the backyard. The howling will be music, not an idea, and therefore will find an appreciative, sophisticated audience.

Aarrkoweenem!

if language is tainted then it will swell in the mouth
we shall be mute and draw pictures to show others
the drawings will be crude at first then swoop and swoon
until the swelling has gone down and then we will eat
more words our faces like ovens over the art

Maybe we should reinvent the ferryman, the boat, even the river, adapt the language to hold the big, bumpy thoughts churning beneath our propellers.

if language is weather
each day until we search silence
if language still bolts like lightning between the teeth

I've got to think things about things. I'm crazy about answers, even wrong ones. I think language can carry more than it thinks. Things happen. Story stirs the white page.

not jello but stew creeping out of the pot
if eyelids twitch from night syllables

Now some thinkers say we must throw plot off the literature boat, toss it a life preserver (call it genre writing). Leave all the more important language free to mill and mull. But I need stories, need water, oars, biceps rising like grain. We must move and imagine ourselves moving, or (sharks) we shall languish in a horrid wet.

if dictionaries pulse like sex
if words pull like disaster
then we must visit them
more often

A Reading

HOLLY IGLESIAS

The poet declares the body didactic; and I yearn for yours, desire sparked by the sight of a girl on a bike, calves pulsing as she pumped up an incline, chest parallel to the road. Child, I long for a bite of you, eight years old, drenched in sweat as you stole away from me, the glee of misdeeds flushing your face. I want to hold you in my mouth, your slick summer neck clamped between my teeth like a newly whelped pup; to know once again the flesh and bones of us before gravity gained momentum. When you were perfect—lash, tendon and toe—and I equally new.

These days, you assemble and re-arrange yourself as if parts were missing. Nails buried beneath acrylic confections one day pale as beer, the next like bruised plums. Your hair disappoints; your breasts a hazard; and you consider the knife and their reduction. *Ach du,* spit on that ancient boot; retain what makes you matter—the dense pounds and lipid pints, the nerve bundles and your blunt, lovely teeth. Or release them to me for safekeeping. I, the failed Empress of Air, my body beginning to slide like layers of an over-iced cake.

Teaching in My Sleep

KATHLEEN KIRK

Tonight again I am
teaching in my sleep
unable to detach
my sharpened feet
from the nest's edge
where my students'
beaks wide open pink
with awe and need
clamor and claw
in peer groups of three

I disengorge the semi
digested worm
of my expertise
into the nearest craw
and rise straight up
screeching and flapping
into black branches
that hide trembling
stars and teach me
how to wake and fly

Teacher Shot by Student, or The Risk of Overstatement

KATHLEEN KIRK

I fail him for submitting
a paper written by his girlfriend
for the same class last quarter and then fall
quarter he walks in and shoots me
but not before I yell
to my students, *Duck! Throw
your books at him!* They do:
a Norton Anthology bruises his forehead.
We will laugh about this later,
I wish. In the expansive moments
we lie there together
on the ashen tiles flecked with mauve,
maroon, navy blue, and teal (I'd never
have known but for this perspective),
I see the bruise gather slowly
on his skin like a dark cloud.
The bullet beside my heart
feels like a gift now, a small
but heavy object of great value,
chosen with some care. *Thank you*
I tell the boy who has taken
my life in return. His lashes
like wings of a wounded moth
struggle to open. When I see
the whites of his eyes, I say,
Live with this, my blood on his hands
now, soaking through to his chest, belly,
spreading past him to the shocked
scuffed shoes of the Lit students
who will track it through this room
and down the halls of their lives.

Introduction to Poetry

SHANNON MARQUEZ MCGUIRE

Walking library aisles two hours, up the PR's, down the PS's, I've gathered
nineteen volumes, slim but voluptuous with phrases. All those images helter-
skelter; the bindings' colors clashing; their grains rubbing, creating friction,
heat; the books' sharp corners biting one another's spines and tearing their ways

through the heavy bottom of the only bag I found, a see-through Walmart bag,
its thin plastine transluscent as a jumbo prophylactic, a jaunty yellow smiley face
shaping the big "O" in this week's slogan: "Rolling back prices at Walmart!"
I'm beaming like a blue-light special. I barely feel the handles that cut into my hand.

I'm in a library in Louisiana, in the market for a feast to feed my unsuspecting guests.
(They signed up for a class; they trust computers and a phone.) Now they'll have
to taste-test every treat that's in my bag. (I've razed the shelves and found new meat.)
Inside the bag, heaped poets tear at one another with sharp words. (Not even the call

numbers are in order.) Auditory images splash into the quiet, dusty air—clashes
and cacophony. Librarians shoosh me. I try a hiss: those books'd better keep it
quiet till we make it out the door. I wonder.... Could they be mad about the bag?
Well, too bad, poets. One more price you pay for publication. Anyway, I'm rolling

back a few prices myself. Listen, Students. Sign up today. You
 could find some
sympathetic soul, stop speaking in clichés. You'll laugh, you'll
 cry, you'll curse.
I swear, you'll die when you read this stuff. (You'll just, kinda
 like, die if you don't.)
You're invited to a feast: Nineteen poets stripped, peeled,
 readied for your devouring

pleasure. Some are a trifle chilly; not a single one's been
 coddled. Several are done
to a turn. One has written downright pickled. A few are truly
 sweet (with natural
sugars only). And mind those two: they're hot and on the very
 verge of creaming.
Ahem. I wipe the sales smile from my face and pile the books
 high on the counter.

A pimply clerk counts up nineteen and shakes his head, then
 piles them high again.
Just a minute, then I stash them in my car. The poets settle in
 and start to chat.
By engine's roar, eighteen poets quiet down and give one
 gentle one the floor.
I listen, and notice that I'm humming—a little alliteration,
 some soft consonance.

Ignoring the Linguist

ROBERT PARHAM

When the professor explained that
the raspberry was, in part, lost,
that is, meaning . . . oh, as he put it:
"The morpheme of 'rasp' is in one sense full,
but we have lost its meaning . . . *berry*,
however, we understand . . ."

                    I think of red
raspberries, fresh in late spring, cream
their tiny sea, as the veranda fills
with the gift of mockingbirds
while I wait for you, that grey bird
doing covers of the quail and the wren.
Fragile as the empty heart
of the raspberry that closes
about it under our tongue . . .
while the light, because it is summer,
refuses to leave.

Reading for the Blind

Kara Provost

for Carolyn Forché

Terrible angels
hover in angles of light,
love us for the way we hold the bodies
of our lovers, swish thick paint on canvas,
set our brains' engines humming;
rage at our failure still
to love all.

You can tell by how she reads
she loves language.
When she speaks, words take substance:
howling throbbing caressing, words pour
out of her mouth as pebbles, silk, wounds, bread.

Slowly, the audience
makes out bits of light
sparkling from silver as her hands
move with her words:
fluttering birds
calling to us,
letting slip through fingers
innumerable griefs.

She sends her voice out into the dark
carefully,
holding words like babies
with still-soft necks.

Her voice feeds
listeners' eyeless vision,
together creating wordpictures.

Reading for the Blind

In the blueness of early morning dreaming
a tatter of sweet jasmine
blooms from ashes of bone and brick.
One day we will learn
how not to make war.

She sends her voice out into the dark
and gets back
all the words ever spoken,
paired with every listener's language: words
soar around her like swallows,
words become eyes
letting us see ourselves
as the angels see us.

The Teacher

Tom Romano

Why do I forget question marks.
I am notorious for it.
My students scoff at me,
"How can you teach English when
you don't punctuate proper?"

I don't teach you anyway, I think,
just lead you like a scout master
and hope you'll dip your hand
into the brook—cold like no
tap water you've ever felt,
let you marvel, a little frightened,
at a snake, mouth agape,
before it darts between rocks,
an image you'll carry for years,
spur you to anger when I won't
stop to let you rest,
even hope you catch poison ivy,
and, as we race up the hill,
urge you on when
you leave me behind,
gasping,
a seeming spear
wedged between my ribs.

Of the absent question mark, I say,
"An innocent, harmless error."
And those of you who aren't smug
point out that I should
extend to you
the same courteous understanding.
I uncap my canteen,
drop to the grass, and,
before I take a long swig,
say, "Why not."

A Case for Literature

DARRELL G. H. SCHRAMM

Peace without the sweat of dance.
No good riddance. A metal bird
with yellow legs beside the white
begonias; a string of opalescent fish
suspended in the stairwell, a swell
of Austin roses that never quite
unfold, a rusted cream can,
a stalk of anise eight feet tall
gone to seed. It's not like that.
Not even the knickerbockers turned
inside out, hanging from the line,
nor snail silver on the Japanese maple.

No. Picture the uprooted, the naked,
on a road of blistering stones.
A darkened room where a father thrusts
home in his male-child. A man
afraid to be touched. Someone hoping,
like most of us, to get it right
this time, next time. A council
that shits on the human spirit. A hospice
of the barely breathing. The things
we'll never understand. Dante
emerging from the Inferno each time
someone reads. The stories we need.

Nostradamus in Heaven

Sarah Sloane

When Nostradamus died and went to heaven one inky July night in 1566, his first concern (after meeting the entrance requirements) was to get a good seat for forthcoming events, not a few of which he had predicted in his book, *Centuries*. So, after his long sickness, the fading of sounds, shedding the body, the tunnel, the light, the greater light, a temporary euphoria followed by endless interviews with insouciant gatekeepers, Nostradamus was issued his heavenly hammock. An incontinent angel told him to make himself at home, so Nostradamus hung his hammock right on the very edge of the big blue sky to see and hear better what happened below.

The first thing Nostradamus saw was not the Renaissance, but was one tiny event in the background of the Renaissance: He saw a crested flycatcher dressing its nest with snake skins—he could see several lengths of the papery husks weaving into the twigs and bark, the loose phantom ends of the snake skins limp in the nest's edge. As he watched the flycatcher weave the nest, Nostradamus soon discovered that he couldn't hear it; in fact, he couldn't hear anything at all, not the flycatcher nor the snake skins rattling, nor, he confirmed, anything happening on earth at all. It was silent as a tomb. Well, that was a change. Distracted only temporarily, Nostradamus soon settled back into his hammock and began to calculate his score in a notebook, keeping track of how many of his predictions came true.

What Nostradamus got right: The Mino-Owari earthquake, Krakatoa, several tsunamis, WWII, the fixed elections of the Pope, Cheezits, global warming, Groundhog's Day, the Kremlin, nitrous oxide, global trading of slaves, Gandhi, the Flatiron Building, shrapnel, dog biscuits.

What Nostradamus got wrong: Mount St. Helen's eruption, dental anatomy, Hinduism, sleeping cars, the date of the first demonstration of obstetric forceps, John Greenleaf Whittier, tennis, the Moog synthesizer, Chinese revolutions, Spinoza, and Egg Watchers (the popular egg substitute).

Score: Roughly even between hits and misses.
Self-Assessment: B+

After a few hundred years, Nostradamus decided it was time to vary his routine, to specialize in the subject of his observations. He would concentrate on continental drift, or take in only those scenes that had to do with dogs, or canteloupe, or the question of pain. He would study thematically. He would witness divorce rates. He would canonize poetry. Yes, he decided finally, yes, he would spend the next thousand years studying poems. So Nostradamus turned his periscope upside-down and peered at the earth until he found a town, a school, a classroom in which all the students were writing poetry. He saw that one girl was doodling in her margins about soft things: honey, feathers, smoke, lambs' ears. A boy was considering the rhyme of *suture* and *future*. The teacher was looking out the window.

Then Nostradamus saw this: A girl fills her fountain pen with vivid blue ink, and her pen leaves blue words that become rivulets flowing down the page. Birds rise from her stream: a yellow hammer, two swifts, a blue tit, a waxwing, and a wheat ear rise from the rivulets and pant after a sluggish, peevish-looking stonechat, circling up into the sky. More Old World songbirds rise from the girl's blue words and pour into the air, flapping their feathers and chattering as they float up towards Nostradamus's preternaturally large eye. Nostradamus rocks in his hammock over our planet as the birds flood towards him singing, their bodies light, their small chests heaving. And for the first time in centuries, Nostradamus hears our mortal words singing back to him again from this half-grown, blue-green, divine, dull world.

Playground

KATE SONTAG

You search the day for inspiration
as it drags by without cause or effect
and come across the wind
sweeping up suddenly through the trees
like a quarrel between two sixth graders
about what the wind looks like
until the trees themselves seem to be arguing
the birch taking the girl's side
saying *you can't see wind*
the aspen siding with the boy
saying *you can see it in the trees*
you agreeing with them both
thinking the girl will grow up to be
a physicist and the boy a painter
believing for a moment
as you watch their shadows die down
with the swings on the empty playground
the trees would give anything to keep
the wind passing through them
distracted now and elsewhere.

PART THREE

Of Reading, Writing, Teaching, Being Taught

Prepositions in Alabama

KEN AUTREY

About Columbus Day, 6th grade, I learned the power
 of lists when Mrs. Hancock held the grammar book
Above our heads and pointed to the prepositions,
 stark and alphabetical. Gesturing
Across the room like an explorer in a painting,
 she vowed we'd have them down in order
After a week's daily drills, able
 to reel them out as smooth as auctioneers.
Against my instinct that the best way
 was to muddle through on guesswork,
Among the others I set my memory to the task,
 rhymeless amid this agonizing litany.
Around nine Friday my turn came first
 (my patronym begins in "A"). I took my stab
At what I knew, "about" to "if" to "on" to "with"
 and didn't drop a syllable.

Upon our shoulders lay the weight of grammar,
 our burden—to find the objects for all words.
Under a cloud of chalkdust we fidgeted
 over the year amid her ranks of facts
Until our heads knocked with the names
 of presidents, rivers, seas, and states.
Toward Easter came the counties of Alabama,
 this time in circuitous order—
To list them on that map that mirrors Mississippi:
 Baldwin, Mobile, up the left side, around
Through Geneva, Covington, Escambia. Even
 our sleep resounded with the catalog
Of Indian tribes—Autauga, Cherokee—and harsher
 names for elder patriarchs—Hale, Wilcox, Pike.
On our memories trudged until June brought us all
 we'd ever need of who, what, when, and where.

Art Lesson

CRAIG CHALLENDER

". . . eschews the quotidian," he was saying.
"That's why it's art." She stopped doodling, looked up.
Professor Bogard—Dr. Bogus—was still
on Yeats: "'The young / In one another's arms'"
(a bifocaled stab her way) "'. . . sensual music . . .
Consume my heart away . . . artifice
of eternity.'" The open watchfob
like a golden eye. A beat. Two.
"'Once out of nature I shall never take
My bodily form from any natural thing. . . .'"

That plummy voice, *doling out Art
to the likes of us,* she thought. But *quote* something—
something, *chew* what? She must have frowned.
Bogus again, right to her chest: "Something
wrong, Miss Smythe?" All eyes on her, fuck
you very much. "No sir. It's just that phrase
you used before the poem, I didn't understand—"
"'Eschew,' perhaps?" The coffee smile. "I'll leave
that one for you. 'Quotidian' is 'commonplace'"
—stereo Bicscratch, sorority smocks,

Tommy Girl blooming the whole room blonde—
"the dailiness of life that drives us mad,
unless redeemed by art's refining fire:
pimples. Parking tickets. The nightly news."
A *click* of fob; his finger traced its swell.
"Desire itself. The quo*ti*dian"—she caught
the second syllable's slight push—
"the bane of our sorry-blank existence. Well.
Class dismissed." The usual male
exodus from English 202,

Art Lesson

Smattering of suck-up from a Kappa Sig
("Yeets is *won*derful, is it too late
to change my topic, Dr. Bogard?" "Miss
Smythe." A folder-filled hand—freckles,
a rivery vein—kept her from sliding by.
"Beneath that attitude's a major screaming
for release. Why fight it? You can't
stay Undeclared forever." *Oh yes
I can,* she thought. *And lay off my syllables,
Buster.* "Well, Dr. Bogard . . ."

"At least drop by sometime and we'll discuss
this poem. It's Yeats's *ars poetica,*
I think." Eyes startlingly raw behind
gold frames. "Just name a time. Even
after hours."
           "'Ars poetica'?" Her way
of easing out, as the myth of Bogard hardened
to a handful of small, sad facts. *He's staring
at my ass* she thought, turned: a smile.
Twin discs of light. "I'll look it up.
So long, Dr. Bogard." Silence.

She never did drop by, but did drop out
of Bogard's class. She repeated 202
(a woman prof, this time). She looked things up.
And, late one evening, saw. The assignment
was Yeats (again!), a weird thing about
circus animals, but the last line
made her whole self resonate:
the foul rag-and-bone shop of the heart.
Heart, Art: tines quivering to single
song. "He got it wrong. We're what we've got."

Her blood hummed with No-Doze details squeezed
from the campus grapevine: love-nest office,
trophy photos, parkside poetry and wine,

creepy e-mail—all flowed past *heart*
like a silent coda. She touched the page, closed
her eyes: Bogard perched on his golden bough,
feeling it melt, trying to sing. A lump
surprised her throat. Social Work. She'd
go that route, do an English minor.
In spite of everything, she liked to read.

Blizzard
Cynthia Miller Coffel

Julie Seaton can't sleep. She's standing in her living room in snowy Oneonta, New York, at midnight, wondering what she'll do, now that she's really resigned—shoved her letter into the principal's box with her head turned as if she could hide what she was doing from herself—now that she's decided to leave this town, and teaching, work she thought she loved, work she'd planned to do since she was little, when she imagined she was a pioneer, leading her students through a blizzard and across the prairies to safety.

It's absurd, Julie thinks as she looks out of the bay windows onto the snowfall, at the Center Street Store with its blue and orange signs announcing "Fresh Seafood/Live Lobsters," and "New York Times Sold Here Daily," and its cardboard Santa, waving on the roof year round. She thinks about her students, the welfare kids and the future marines, the ones who wrote sad messages on their desks: "Death is once," "Fuck the Rich," and inked-in, intricate drawings of naked women with their legs spread wide. She thinks about big tattooed Beckwith, who cried when he lost his $.99 folder, and little Lynette Pittsley, who never took a bath because her father demanded sex when she did, and Damon, whose soft red hair curled against her pink satin K-Mart blouse as she sang in the rock band she'd started: He's My Salvation.

Julie looks at the dove gray sky, at a red light on the corner, at snow falling on a Madonna in the yard next-door. She's abandoning Anita, she thinks, and her boyfriend Michael, who'd pull month-old, wrinkled homework papers out of a grocery sack when he stopped by the class; he was living in an Oldsmobile out on Route 12, he said, and Anita was set up in a shack, where she held their baby Darren in one arm and a rifle in the other and shot at the rats that dragged in under the door.

Peace, Julie thinks, I need peace, and I never imagined this, the poverty of their lives, my helplessness. In front of her sit crates marked "oranges" and "Coors," crates she'll fill now with all the stuff of her last two years: the nineteenth-century walking dress she worked on nights, pieces pinned into tissue papers; that stack of books on the ironing board; her disassembled loom; and the purple corduroy hearts drooping over her what-not shelf; she'll sew those hearts into a new dress, once she's away from this town, away from teaching, away from these students who need too much.

She looks out at the snow—almost a blizzard, now, really—and she imagines herself leading her students through it and across the prairies to safety and she imagines herself living far, far away from here, away from her failures, working at a different, less important job, escaping as her students can't, and she thinks, I'll never get to sleep.

Art Elective

STEPHEN COREY

Reflex of memory thrusts
the strong-voweled name *Rouault*
out through my lips as I walk
the hall of my daughter's school
and sight his poster on the wall—
the blocky reds and browns
surrounded by swaths of black,
the squat figures angry
yet somehow sanctified.
I am reminded of style,
how it is rarely taught
but never mistaken once learned,
how I came to it in high school
through luck of scheduling, through Art
Appreciation class—that lone elective
slotted among the requirements.

Old Miss Proctor, green smock
spattered to stringy rainbows,
walked the room like a Pollock miniature.
Her hunched back and wizened face,
the long tables in place of desks,
the full wall of windows—
at first, the class seemed a kindergarten
break, a ball-and-wire cartoon,
Miró amid the testing and the bells.

But Amy was there beside me,
our knees touching beneath the table
we shared in the back-right row.
Our loving scholastic war,
three years old, had never been
so serious and gently fierce
as in those months we learned to sense

the bronze and glow of Rembrandt, to see
the soft-toned lumps of apples and hills—
almost interchangeable, almost alive—
in the many-angled lightings of Cezanne.

The rest of the school was so carefully lit
to protect itself and all of us
from the little darks we were, or might become;
but in Art Appreciation
the dark became the learning space,
holding back the regular light
so the slides could shine and brood
on the luminescent screen above us.
My fingertips were on Amy's thigh,
coming up under her skirt to the edge
where stocking met skin, stunning
border—her hand on me showing
what my hand was doing for her.

Miss Proctor at the bright screen's edge,
pointer and fingers reaching out
to the special blush of blue
that meant Vermeer, "That will mean Vermeer,"
she said, "until the end of the world."
Here, removed from corridors
lined by dull green lockers,
van Gogh's fiery hills and pinwheels
swirled above the Thirteen Colonies,
the rubbery frogs, the cosines, and the verbs—
and this, we came to know, is style:
the heart of a hand and eye,
knowable though unpredictable,
the shapes and shades we acquire
both with and against our wills.

As if need were impediment to learning,
our careful parents lectured us in love—
how it was still a choice for the young,

Art Elective

something not yet hardened by necessity.
But from Blake's acid-etched flames and flowers
arose the palpable words we sought:

You never know what is enough
unless you know what is more than enough.

While others dawdled and stalled
as if nothing here were tangible,
Amy and I sought perfect scores.
Hour by hour after school
we studied the paintings and sculpture again,
studied the curious notes we'd taken
with our free hands in the dark:
a dozen grids by Mondrian,
his primary colors ruled like cloth
exposed by a microscope;
Gauguin's brown and solid bodies,
ominous and awkward paradise.
And Miss Proctor there at our shoulders,
pressing us even with diction:
"Each piece and detail," she said,
"becomes a synecdoche of style."

For just one week she made us
artists, workers in the crafts we observed.
Chalk on heavy paper was my choice,
symbolic abstraction my excuse
for a hand not linked with eye:
a thick, red cross hung high
against blackened air, purple hills
set far below; a jagged graph-line, green,
descending through the cross, moving
left to right into the hills.
The title: "History of Man."
Our final day I abandoned the work,
slashed it with spirals of chalk.
Miss Proctor took it up, championed

its power—swirls and all—to the class.
Amy's thigh gave pressure to mine.
I sat silent, took credit, knowing
Miss Proctor did not believe in accident.
(Her first day's words: *I am an artist.
My name is Florence.*)

I know a man of superb intelligence
who cannot bring himself to eat
a strawberry, although he loves the taste.
As a child he was stricken
by the clear resemblance of strawberries
to his uncle's pocked and bulbous nose;
four decades have not lessened his fear,
his sense of immoral desire. . . .

I watch this poster of Rouault
but see my friend's perverse distress.
I would wish that nose away, would change it
to the breast of my friend's finest lover,
would give him the piling up, the layering,
concocted of dream upon resonant dream—
the writhings of fact made real.

Chalk Dust and Urban Renewal

Trista Cornelius

A memory: *a long, cavernous classroom. The teacher stands at the front in a tweed jacket and thick reflecting glasses. "Do we agree then that summary is different from analysis?" The hum of the overhead projector is the loudest sound in the room. A young girl draws umbrellas at the bottom of her paper and looks out at the plum winter sky. The minute-hand on the clock clicks as it passes twelve. Time and air turn into thick, cold gel.*

Room 343. Sun heats up half the room. Cityscape windows glow orange with construction dust and frail air. Pigeons scratch and strut at dare-devil heights. Silhouettes of heads bend over last-minute work and tilt toward each other in conversation about weekend movies, an impending divorce, and daycare. Heavy particles of chalk cling to rubber soles and travel in ghost-like trails that vanish near the door. The dirt-like smell of chalk marks shed from slick chalkboards chafes my throat.

"Good morning" I say and roll a piece of chalk in my palm.

Fossil-like grit splits my cuticles with its dry thirst. The strong, clean white pulls me toward the blackboard. I strike the black surface and make the first mark, securing a student's comment in language, in art on this surface, honoring ideas in words, preserving them in print in our visual memories. The sun catches pieces of chalk floating over me like the slivers of splintered glass being crushed three stories below. Feathery white powder lands on my black sweater, cloaking me as part of the room, chalkboard camouflage.

Laughter.

I've misspelled a word. The letters are thick-white, bold, but crooked. They convey my feeling for this class, for their thoughts and my thrill of being there, in front of them, transferring their ideas like a conduit. The crisp fraying of chalk on the board marks time to the beat of class discussion, pounding through silent pauses and marching on past the text and into our lives.

It's rumored that a sociology professor eats chalk in front of his class. A bizarre concept, but I understand the urge to look out into a small pond of faces, feel the electricity of inquiry, of change and transformation, and to want to taste the process of learning, like a powerful spice.

I imagine taking a small bite, appreciating the crisp snap and grit, and, like communion, passing it around for everyone to taste.

my last glad summer

PHEBE DAVIDSON

my last glad summer of lust
and cream, I read seed catalogs
and dreamed spring gardens

and a student told my class
how Jefferson built a great snake fence,

and how he was a man of large
unsleeping passions
and how he loved to ride

the wide Virginia spring
and the high blue folded hills

and the young sudden hunger
of her voice
made lilies bloom beneath my skin

Bar Mitzvah Lessons

MARVIN DIOGENES

I took bar mitzvah lessons from Mr. Bodzin,
he of the bullet head, silvered gristle
at the temples. He taught me to decode
the musical notations
sprinkled among the Hebrew letters.
Most were easy to remember, easy
to sing—sequences of squiggles
soon familiar as the Beatles' "Paperback Writer."

There were one or two harder
symbols, misshapen corkscrews
demanding vocal arabesques. Mr. Bodzin sang
these notes in his indignant
graveled baritone, and I parroted
him with my squeaky tenor.
He sang again, letting me know
I was off. Sometimes I got close
enough, and then we would go on.

On the day I became a man
I did not see Mr. Bodzin
at shul, though I heard his judgment later:
another student still in training reported
that Bodzin had pronounced me
adequate, faltering on the more artistic
notes, the double loops, the breath-sapping axles.
Everyone else was proud.

I remember Mr. Bodzin's bullet head,
his irritated melody, his grudging
obeisance to a God who craved
the voices of boys,
his knowing assessment
of how far I had to go.

Crescendo

KATHERINE M. FISCHER

He is the man to whom I would eventually give many of the best years of my life. There is something about his demeanor: I expect him to walk into a human outline here in the foyer declaring, "Good Evening, Ladies." I'd begged to take piano lessons, but I had Ted Mack's Amateur Hour in mind, not Alfred Hitchcock. "You must be Ralph Ferber," mother says. "And this is my student," he responds, glancing solemnly at me.

Student? I had pictured myself wearing an ivory crinoline dress, pink bows in my hazelnut hair, as I sat with fingers poised on the keys, spinning gossamer notes floating from the raised lid of the baby grand to parents, friends, kings and queens who nodded proclaiming, "The next Chopin, the next Dvořák." But studying? Like school? Not likely.

I follow Ralph Ferber into the parlor and sit fidgeting on the bench. He moves purposefully, lunges, picks up the green chair, and sets it down next to my bench, "Close enough to see your fingers now." Every Friday evening for the next eight years, he lunges, hoists the chair, and positions it beside the bench. Arpeggios, sonatas, and pages of scales fill my Fridays along with Mr. Ferber's revisions: "Lift the wrist," "Make that a sharp," and "Try it pianissimo."

Winter Fridays when he rings the doorbell, he wears a thin gray wool scarf with one pocket. My sister and I giggle about this later as we fall asleep, but in time I come to set great store by that pocket. Were Mr. Ferber to arrive wearing some red scarf without a pocket, I am sure we would all cease breathing. Were he to open the door without ringing or enter the parlor and plop into the loveseat instead of the "Ferbs chair," I know the earth would stop spinning. In his very regularness, I learn to take chances, to risk imbalance, to fall in love with learning. . . and with teaching, the kind that occurs outside the classroom.

Endless Sunday recitals in August with my fingers slipping off the keys, I miss so many notes that my recital is more silence than sound. But in silence, I learn that the performance is nothing compared to the worth of working hard on something I will never be the best at. I learn that persistence by the teacher can engender persistence in the student.

Years later, we meet again at mother's house. He rings the doorbell, strolls into the parlor, lunges, and hoists the green chair to its spot. The most important lessons I learn from Ralph Ferber are not crescendos or syncopation—at least not in music. I learn about being a teacher one-to-one (later to serve me in writing conferences with students), the art of being consistent, and that teaching is always under revision. Most of all, I learn that the world will not end if the student flubs a recital . . . or if the teacher spends part of a lesson moving chairs.

My Bad

Douglas Goetsch

Ignore her, they said.
They were veterans. They'd seen a lot
of black kids on the last day of school
pleading with, then threatening their
white teachers, who had pleaded with them
all term to get to class and do their work,
and this girl standing at the gymnasium door
was no different. So I concentrated
on keeping my dribble, hitting
the open man, getting back on D,
as she stood there calling *Mr. Halpern,*
me running full-court with math
teachers, hairy, angular, bearded, bald,
not one of us a match for the boys
who dunked on the bent rims of her neighborhood.
She stayed in that doorway, saying my name
until I knew she was right,
that she'd *passed* the class,
that it was my bad—I'd confused her
with another girl when filling out my grades.
She'd be going to summer school
unless I did something then and there.
But I didn't.

I could say I was young,
and maybe I wanted just once
to leave a mistake, the way men
leave women. I wanted the truth
to take a day off. I wanted
to play basketball, to get a good look
at the hoop, and when I did,
when I hit the open J that
won the game, I looked over

and the girl was gone.
Fixed in her mind
is a snapshot of how I run,
or fake, the sweat stains
I make on a white shirt.

Puttyroot and Stopcock

David Graham

Old Mr. What's His Name was always good
for a hoot in study hall: installing
himself solemnly behind the oak desk,
he'd open the unabridged with a random
heave, and proceed to scan a single page
through the whole hour, his bald crown beaconing
unutterable dullness down the rows
where we sat all fidgety and sidelong,
scooting notes down the aisles, miming
mile-wide yawns at his ponderous head.
Imagine, reading a dictionary!
—as if it burned with a novel's heat,
as though the gutter cleft gave out some
earthly perfume we were too rabid to know.
The only fragrance *we'd* admit to our dreams
abided in airy strangeness
beneath a cheerleader's upkicked skirts.

Ah, Mr. Whoever, for the good part
of three decades now I've followed the light
from your luminous skull, browsing *stopcock*
and *puttyroot*, pondering the shades
of desire in *beguile, entice, inveigle*
and *lure*—in short, I've entered with open eye
(and here I mean to dwell till the book shuts)
the wondrous fog of your wide ignorance.

First Piano Teacher

AVA LEAVELL HAYMON

Earnest Mrs. Clinkscales, the first piano teacher.
Who tried so hard, whose nose ran all winter
and always an ironed handkerchief up her sleeve.
Curve your fingers! Phrase from the wrist!
Salty three inch white busts of Haydn and Bach
sat on her dusted piano, Brahms in the breakfront
near a perfume bottle from the 1900 World's Fair,
her only trip. A careful woman. Conscientious.
Emphasized sight reading and the metronome.
There are some things a boy has got to know
whether he wants to or not. Sometimes the night
before his lesson she'd dream a cave is discovered,
huge as Kansas, with unthinkably tall rooms
—she must have eaten something spicy—
in one of the rooms a cadmium yellow mineral
that would brighten up just about anything.

Poor Mrs. Clinkscales, linen dickey
pressed flat as a board, her commitment
to five finger exercises and Beethoven harmonics,
dynamics clearly specified if you look
right below the line, her satisfaction
in the rectitude of a piano, where pitches hold
and cannot slip and slide around.
And how could his mother dress him so!
He'd put on airs for the rest of his life!

After an Old Picture of School House Children

WILL HOCHMAN

(When they paid teachers with livestock)

Attending cures snobbery and mind
like bacon, the insufferable arrogance
of ideas exploding in the finally
understood guidance of a storybook pig
who ultimately teaches reading
to generations of prairie kids
frying in the beautiful
unconscious fat of no TV.
So much surrounds this shack
that isn't there—in a picture
tube of time swirling like cotton candy
I see something almost escapable,
something slight, a sliver of students
as young eye glasses
to see school through brightly,
and maybe magnify learning's focus
so much later in their lives.
The camera can't gather their gazing
and their gleaming faces don't make it
any easier to imagine me the teacher
clicking, clucking, then reprimanding
the memory lovingly, with arms still akimbo.
So much grows beyond the frame
it's fruitless for this humble idea
orchard to expect a harvest sweet
enough to provide anything beyond
the point that there could have been more
and surely was.

The Autobiography of Tulips
HOLLY IGLESIAS

The book's overdue, but I can't let it go; sigh at the mere sight of that gap where it sat on the shelf all those years before I checked it out. A slim volume no wider than the space between my brother's front teeth. My love for her grows, page after page after page.

Mary Krummenacher? Mary! Nuns eternally calling me by my baptismal name, that humdrum name, intolerant of nickname nonsense. I'm not a bad girl (though I' d like to sing the back-up on Blue Suede Shoes) but I cannot deliver this book report; won't cough it up. No. *The Autobiography of Tulips* remains my very own secret. Give me a big fat zero, lower my blasted average. She's mine.

Imagine! Firm, waxy cups on long stems—red, yellow, liver purple—melting in the heat. I used to think I loved tulips because we were Dutch; because four delftware couples, clogged and kissing beneath a windmill, lined my grandparents' mantelpiece. Then Grandma burst into tears one day in the middle of dusting the knickknacks, saying that during the war somebody threw a brick through the window of Doodle's drugstore, screaming *Kaiser lover!* and they never called themselves German again. *Oh, kid, they called us barbarians.*

Every spring they took the train to Michigan to see the fields of tulips, to buy tulip placemats and tulip-bulb salt-and-pepper shakers with HOLLAND in bright red letters. I wonder: what makes somebody want to be a tourist? Sister Rose Campion thumps her desk for attention, orders us to decline *granum*. I just want to go home and write my own book: *The Dictionary Unraveled*.

Deep Blue

HOLLY IGLESIAS

Seeds extracted one by one from *la cascara*, the membrane sharp around the star-core. In the place between poetry and prose; before pressure, the germ of Apple unexpressed between two teeth; then the clamping that releases a bitter essence and the savor of almond.

Inside *El Rincón Wilma* the slatted shade. A row of stools, two men smoking return my stare. Outside, gazing through the window that opens to the sidewalk, always outside. An orange cooler, silver paper-cup dispenser, thimbles of *café cubano*. Thwacking old grounds into the trash, tamping new into the vise: *espresso*. And pan slathered yellow, browning on the *parrilla*, a glass box of *croquetas* and *panqué Jamaica*, sizzling oil, the crackle of carmelized sugar. Beans thickening: *empapado, aguado—isleño* sounds, slurring pain with sweet. *Toma chocolate, paga lo que debe.*

Eyes moisten for Martí, the poet-doctor crying his passion down the years for all of them. *¡La Patria, que viva!* The song of it lost in the 90-mile crossing, the refrain reduced to sentimental pap. *Yo soy un hombre sincero, de donde crece la palma.* A pride of con artists resting under the shade of an ancient grudge. *Oye, es la candela.*

Sister Valerie Ann, a Sister of Loretto at the Foot of the Cross, her veil clamped under headphones in the language lab, the full length of her habit canting toward our accents. *Azul* and *platano* and *catarro* and *jueves* stumbled over our tongues, plaid-skirted midwestern girls who dreamt of swarthy *Pablos* and lust. Friday afternoon mixers, girls dancing with girls until the guys had tanked up enough to jump in and do the Jerk and lipsynch, *Going back to Miami; going back to my girl.*

The *viejos* mouth their cigars, and I envy them their *medias casino,* their hair pomade. *El exilio soy yo, mi hermano.* They read me impassively through a wall of smoke: outside, full sun, shadowless. *Guayaberas* damp, the mix of contempt and desire souring the starched fabric as they assess my flesh, search for the *lomita* of my ass, for cleavage and the cinch of a waist.

The softest water here. Languid nights, days of inescapable light. The quick and piercing stars. And the fabled pendant moon over Miami.

I order toast and *café con leche,* the waitress staring blankly; the men behind her in the dark shift their gaze into empty cups. They too hear but take no meaning; language and body don't match. Though the accent in my mouth is theirs, the words fall like soot, senseless and flimsy. They hear with their eyes, *los viejos fumando* in the slatted shade.

A bank of orchids. The farmer's market hard against traffic on Ponce de Leon. A woman, heavily braceleted, vaulted tall on stilettos, halts before the display. She fingers an airborne root, strokes the plush of one vulval bloom. Squeals, ¡*Ay honey, está to die for!*

Amphibians Have Feelings Too

GERALD LOCKLIN

There was this fine guy named Steve Odin
and I haven't seen him for many years
but we taught together fifteen years ago
when we were just starting out in graduate school.

The other day I was correcting a freshman paper
which contained many sentence fragments
and I thought of Steve,
because that year he had a kid who kept writing
sentence fragments, and so Steve kept scrawling
FRAG in the margin of the papers,
and the kid never came in for a conference,
he just kept writing sentence fragments
and Steve kept scrawling FRAG in the margin.

Then the last day of the semester rolled around
and after everyone else had left
this student came up to the desk and said,
"Mr. Odin, there's just one thing I'd like to ask you."

"Sure. What is it?"

"Why have you been writing FROG on my paper
all semester?"

Second Apartment, First-Year Teacher

CLAUDIA MONPERE MCISAAC

Just one grocery bag but it was heavy
and I stumbled on the landing,
bumped against the polite young English
major's door when the barking began—
dog but not dog, half scream, half growl,
her voice shouting *down, Spot, down*
and the same voice yelping a reply.
Next door the man beating his girlfriend
and downstairs the nervous law student
who stepped out of his shower one
morning to find his upstairs neighbor peeing
in his toilet. *Why are you taking a shower
in my bathroom?* asked the upstairs neighbor,
a retired physics professor, eyes
perpetually moist and yellow. *Might I ask,
instead,* said the law student, *why you
are peeing in my toilet?* The student kept
books and the physicist kept snakes, two boas
loose in the building, ending their dry
coil in the plumbing like those urban
myths that prove you really should
look before you sit. A bat
in the lobby. Flames nibbling
the hallway curtains. I was teaching
Poe, feeling sick at the creepiness
but it was good fodder for my students.
A new teacher uses whatever she can.
Every week was Halloween and
I was doling the stories out like candy.
When I noticed a smell, sweet
like cinnamon rolls but with a uriney sharpness,
my first thought was maybe the physicist's dead
and his body's rotting inside
and won't that be the story that takes the cake.

Second Apartment, First-Year Teacher

We all joked—
the law student, the beaten wife,
the English major. And I saved the details
of the warning tape around his door
because it turned out he'd been experimenting
with radioactive materials, and I
saved the details of the smell
ricocheting down the stairs as they carried his body out.
As I told my students this story
I knew it would be the last one and wondered
when it's too late to ask forgiveness.

Spring. The English major sews
all night. I hear
the needle's frantic whir
chudit-chudit-chudit-chudit.
China shatters against the wall.
Frantic splashes. Bowls and plates, demitasse cups
brought over from Germany
by her grandmother. I think of how no
word is right—not *smash, splinter, crash, shatter.*
Not *man,* not *woman.*
She won't answer my knocks but comes out
slowly, flinging off each article
of hand-sewn clothing as she walks down the stairs
naked into the Berkeley streets
until she is a polite brown scream
in early morning. And I remember
sipping thick coffee once from her green
and gold china and at the cup's bottom
a clutch of yellow roses.

Teacher's Lounge

BILL RANSOM

At the bell you hobble to your corners
a certain fog muffles the stamps and jeers.

You slump on your stools: your red
spider eyes glitter and cringe in the dark.

The challenger bobs and paws
his vague form grunts through the shadows.

Skylights dissolve these thick webs of smoke
that settle on your shoulders and arms.

You do not hear the bell, your cornerman,
the spit-faced referee. You stand when you see

something like a towel flutter down something like hope,
or like a child spinning helpless in the ring.

Rehabilitating Joseph Adams

SCOTT SIMPSON

They caught him with the pictures—
drawings in ink
he'd done during free hour
holding the notebook up
close to his face
like he might be
writing his mother
or doing homework

The pictures had come
that night
after the first session
with her
he couldn't forget her
fingers, the one nail
broken, and he'd wondered
how she broke it
that's what he was thinking
when she asked him
*Would you like to talk
about why you're here
Joe?*
not *Cadet Adams*
not *Private*
but *Joe*
and he couldn't talk
but he met her eyes
her blue eyes
her soft smile
and the pictures
just came to him
all night
and he tried pressing them
out of his eyes

with his palms
but he loved
the pictures
in which he loved
her
and she, him

so he placed them
on the paper
during free time
so he could return to them
whenever
so they wouldn't
be lost
and he wondered again
how she broke that
fingernail, some tenderness
swelling his throat,
he planned to take it gently into
his hands, kiss her
knuckles
smell the perfume
of her closeness
and hold her

so he wrote at the bottom
Miss Hayes, Ma'am
this private loves you
Ma'am,
this private dreamed
all night of you
Miss Hayes, Ma'am
and this here is what
he dreamed, Ma'am
could he see you
sometime
Ma'am?

They've caught him with the pictures
Drill Instructor Brucker
shouting, *What is this
Cadet Adams?*
*M-m-m some mighty pretty
pictures—*
*You think I should
give these lovelies
to Miss Hayes?*

No Sir

*No Sir, Cadet
No sir-ee
I think you should
give them to Miss Hayes
Don't you Cadet?
Don't you think an
invitation
should be hand-delivered?*

*No Sir
Please Sir, this Private
will throw them away
Sir, he was
out of line, Sir*
and Brucker lowers
his voice
through a smile, chuckles
*You're damn right
Joe, out of line*
and Brucker turns,
moves to the door
*But I think I will
show them to her, after all
Miss Hayes'll get a laugh
out of a prick
like you, Adams*

and Cadet Adams,
still at attention
closes his eyes
sees no more pictures
of Miss Hayes—
only Brucker
Brucker laughing
Brucker turning
Brucker blood-red
Brucker, Brucker, dead

Spatial Relations
LEONORA SMITH

> "...all true poems are written in the fifth dimension..."
> —Colin Wilson: *The Occult* (citing Robert Graves)

Remember the geometric forms on aptitude tests—
Combinations of cubes and cones the questions asked us

to upend and rotate, or turn inside out, or trapezoids
and rhomboids we were to fold so we could choose

the figure they would make, assembled? I fingered
six sides of my pencil, trying to squeeze my eyes

smart for this piece of engineering zanier
than building a dress (matching right sides to right,

and trying to imagine it turned inside out and backward
from the way it was in my hands to become a pocket

or a sleeve). When my brain failed from parallelograms
that might fold in to make a prism, I blinked up

at the other eighth graders hunched over booklets
spread on the cafeteria tables, all of us spaced

two seats apart so we couldn't cheat and claim an aptitude
that wasn't ours: Van who's dead now, Richard

in his immaculate white pants, Cookie
finger-pressing pleats in her cheerleader skirt, Eva

who couldn't read, biting off bits of her eraser
and examining them in her palm as if they were the test.

Then the monitor chalked zero over a smudged five
to show minutes left, said "time!—booklets closed,"

and I looked down and tried to take the edges up,
to stick and paste one tab into one slit, as if the pattern of
    lines

were a child's punch-out cardboard house. My eyes
stuttered and my mind stuttered back. And, at once,

I *could* see the figure they would be, as the plane shapes
folded themselves in and stood up on the page

in solid geometry—and a little, but not at all clearly—
the spaces—neither figure nor margin—

which hung in the blurred wakes of their folding.

"... Water and the Word Suicide"

KATE SONTAG

While the rest of us were asleep
    Jason Anthony Cotter drifted till morning.
From this university cafeteria's complex
    of glass & steel you can follow the icy current

a short distance to where two days ago
    his body was dragged out of the freezing
Mississippi-bound water. I come here often
    for coffee with colleagues or anonymously

to study the panorama of river through trees.
    Today I'm imagining a student—not one of mine,
but someone who wrote poems he showed
    to his writing instructor—standing on the bridge

around midnight. He was twenty, Black, from Chicago
    and left in his room "poetry and miscellaneous jottings
with references to water and the word suicide."
    His teacher got angry when she read the news.

Someone said she'd recognized his picture
    in the paper then stormed out of the building.
Will she catch herself in the elegiac half-light
    of this afternoon, scanning her memory

of his lines for some clue, some connection
    he wanted her to make? The harder it snows
the more like an old photograph this view
    of the Iowa becomes. Two weeks ago

starlings began going crazy in willows and oaks
    along the bank. It's hard to describe the sound
they make each year before migrating, huddled
    in branches, about to take their lives into their wings.

Diction Lesson

Patricia Valdata

A writing workshop, held in a tent
on the last warm day of summer.
The instructor talks of diction
when four black and white chickens
stroll inside. Plucking at the dirt,
three hens cluck their way out,

the fourth trapped in the forest
of yellow plastic chairs. Nervous noises
in the wattled throat draw student
thought from the abstract to the concrete:
    This chicken is a barred Plymouth Rock hen.
    This chicken lays a brown-shelled egg.

And this chicken paces an uneasy circle,
looking for the Waterloo lawn, so we
sidle our plastic chairs apart to give
her an escape route, while our teacher
discusses the merits of moving from
the general to the specific.

Part Four

Advice and Observations

Compulsion

Jane Barnes

Yes, you will, you will
write down what you hear:
crisp pages being turned by a putative hand,

and voices raised in the outer room,
rolling gently up and down
in the currents of air from an open door,

mechanical clicks and hums,
the little clatter of latches closing,
the "tock" of paper

shunted to and from copier trays,
and the closer "scritch" of pen
making these lines.

What does it mean?
What does it signify, this listening,
when the ear confers no sense?

Only to receive the data, to store it
temporarily or forever,
with questionable future access—

this is all.

Flat Out

JACQUELINE BRICE-FINCH

A fine weariness
penetrates
to my bones.

My body
craves
a sleep
not possible
until
the last word
is proofed.

My eyes strain
and tear slowly
as they focus
on the page,
then the screen.

I am too tired
even
to speak
distinctly,
settling
for a slurring
discourse
of frustrating
communication.

The tantrum
of the overtired child
I exhibit
in an irascible attitude
of impatience,
frustration

Flat Out

While getting
the work
done
at a pace
so
lethargically
slow
that the effort
seems
in vain.

Finally
the voice of reason
penetrates:
Gon' home
chile,
an' get
some rest.

Advice to a Young Poet

KELLY CHERRY

To catch a poem
to seize it
like something falling

or flying,
word-wings—

and it slips
through your fingers,
a piece of light
or shadow—

alertness,
you need, and
patience.

The poem,
when trapped,
must be treated tenderly.

It may be observed and tagged.

Then release it
into freedom,
let it live

on its own terms.

Reply

Helen Degen Cohen

A teacher, who is also my friend,
just told me
that I may not use
the word reply in a poem.
I said a friend, because he is one.
But last year it was beauty.
And ten years ago, love.

And maybe he is right.

Only look, I am at this moment
walking the longest walk
under the bluest sky,
a walk which began with no sky at all
and may end the same,
and look, I, at this moment, see
a bird I have never seen before,
though I think it once flew restless
between the walls of my dream:

up there, just an ordinary bird
doing an extraordinary thing,
flapping its wings *Reply! Reply! Reply!*
soaring, and again, *Reply! Reply! Reply!*
as if only for the joy of it,

the sound coming not from its throat,
but the beating of those wings.

I know that one day
those wings will steady and slow
and, near silence, leave behind them
a new sound for beauty and love
and even more ancient things,

like, O *my teacher, my teacher,*
before he dies.

Adjunct

BROCK DETHIER

With a Bartleby of Arts
and a doctorate in Denial,
I've survived four Chairs,
three Deans and
six or eight Directors.
Student butts beyond count
have squirmed in my one chair.
My floor is white with dead letters.
My recycling box is always full.

Take the stairs to the top—
no Penthouse here—
hang lefts until you see the end.
Where the hallway dies, that's me—
King of the Dead End,
Master of Intermission,
Sultan of Sour Grapes.

The ceiling is low,
the walls very high,
there's a window into a shaft.
The perfboard's covered
with crayoned monsters,
tales of freak beheadings,
the shelves are filled with
books thrown out by those who rose.

Read the screed
outside my door,
genuflect before you knock—
in a year if you're lucky
you'll be on the tenure ladder
at the College of Great Benefits
while I'm teaching your replacement
how to climb.

Not to Be

BROCK DETHIER

Carve your name in the paper
Don't hide behind "be"
Broadcast who what and when
Seize a stand.

Subject verbs object
The quick agent acts
Insist on fresh verbs
Reject canned.

Assert, say "I do"
Not "I was done to."
Swim the stream, surf the flow
Fight the drift.

Pep up your prose and
Wake up your readers
Treasure strong verbs
Share the gift.

Produce

DARRELL FIKE

"Oh, send along a half-dozen fresh ones,"
the editor said, meaning my poems, as if
I grew them out back in neatly mulched rows,
sprouting daily and trained to follow a trellis,
hanging ripe and ready to be gathered
bunched or bundled, whenever I have the need.

Later, rummaging through what I had on hand
—leftovers, odds and ends saved and forgotten—
as mysterious as unmarked freezer food,
I found five that would not shame me
and in vain I sought for a satisfying sixth,
the last to make his easy half-dozen.

Giving up to errands, in the supermarket
I scanned the faces of other shoppers
in hopes of stealing a quick poem
from the fear in an eye or the secret in a smile,
but all I found was the coffee I like on sale
and two for one cottage cheese with chives.

Then around the corner I was basket
high in the garden of aisle twenty-three,
bunches of broccoli and bags of carrots
begging to have their stories told, bananas
longing for metaphor, melons suggesting
simile, red potatoes sly and winking.

Wildflower Composition

MELISSA GOLDTHWAITE

Spring: I make a chart, tape every weed
I know to cardboard, label and memorize.
Every two weeks, I wade

into the garden, searching for weeds.
In late May, I can see
only dandelions and grasses,

too focused on the familiar
like the one who knows commas
and fragments but nothing

about organization and structure.
Mid-June, I meet thistles, prickly greens
with spine-tipped leaves and purple burrs.

I hold below the florets, follow stem to root
and pull near the dirt. It's the tracing back,
a kind of revision that satisfies,

knowing the shape and feel—
what doesn't work. I see weeds
I can't name, know the feel

isn't right; flowerless greens should
never wind around yarrow, violets,
trillium. Truth is, books

can't always name the difference
between weed and wildflower, what to keep,
what to cut. It's knowing the composition

of your own garden, standing back,
looking, sometimes waiting for flowers
or walking barefoot, testing your own ground.

Just Guessing: A Little Lecture on Ambition
David Graham

> "Rilke was a *jerk*."
> Berryman

Rainer Maria Rilke never worked a day
in his life. He paced the battlements
listening for angelic instruction, leaving
wife and child to scramble for bread in Paris.
He wheedled paper and ink money from rich pals.

Remember this, kids, as you swoon in the lecture hall
or bend to your solo ovals of lamplight,
pondering. Angels never sing *get a job!*
but maybe all your spooked fathers are right,
advising pre-med, glaring down their bifocals
at your GPAs. You could do worse, I swear,
than close the yearbook upon those scrawny verses
I myself have called promising, which your roommate
doesn't understand, and your girlfriend reads
solemnly without a peep. *You're* not a jerk,
I know, but why tempt fate? It would take
the rarest soul to inoculate himself against
angelic blurtings. Don't think Rilke *knew*
his own genius. Don't for a moment suppose
he could reckon the cost of missing his daughter's wedding
because the fit was on him. I swear,
Rilke had no idea he was destined
for all the anthologies and textbooks,
for translation into dozens of tongues,
for epigraphs and legends and tours of his old haunts.
No: like you, like me, Rilke was just guessing.

Creative Writing at Jefferson Correctional Institution

Amorak Huey

Here are the rules:
No weapons, guns or drugs.
Don't ask the women
about their crimes.
Don't agree to bring
anything in or take anything out.
Get the chaplain's approval
before chanting
or speaking in tongues.

Rules are essential in a twenty-acre
compound surrounded by fences,
rolls of razor wire,
flat-eyed guards watching
from corner towers,
rows of low gray buildings,
a writing class in a library
where the shelves are waist-high
so there's nothing to hide behind.

So we minded our business,
tried to teach within the rules,
avoided speaking in tongues,
bringing nothing in, taking nothing out
except all those poems and stories
written on prison-issue paper
with prison-issue pencils,
soft-gray and smudging at the touch.

Rules of Conduct:
Colored Elementary School, 1943

ALLISON JOSEPH

Watch your language, say words right.
Use education as your tool.
Keep every anger curled in tight.

You won't achieve through force or might,
won't rise above through being cruel.
Watch your language, say words right.

Avoid forbidden streets at night,
stay far from dope and alcohol.
Keep every anger curled in tight.

Speak only when you're called and act polite;
don't dare to miss one day of school.
Watch your language, say words right.

Don't be the child who aches to fight,
the one who yearns to break the rules.
Keep every anger coiled in tight.

Live proud, although you are not white.
Don't let them see you act a fool.
Watch your language, say words right.
Keep every anger coiled in tight.

quo vadis, m.f.a.?

GERALD LOCKLIN

do you remember how bartleby the scrivener
felt about his period of employment
in the dead letter office?

that's how i felt this spring
screening a hundred highly qualified
    applications
for a single one-year, non-tenure-track
    lectureship
in creative writing.

Seven Fables of Teaching and Learning

Hans Ostrom

1. Magpie

When I was six years old, I met Magpie in woods beside a creek. I got close. He didn't fly, a lesson in itself. "Kid," he said, "we know only what we remember. You won't know why you'll hold my image all your life." Classic checkerboard floors, contract law, nuns' habits, zebras, bar-codes, bifurcated thinking, and film noire: subjects Magpie helped me understand even after I had graduated, magna cum feathers, from woods into more knowing.

2. Bad Dog

When I was eleven, Bad Dog bit me. "That will teach you," he growled. "Don't trust anybody, number one, and number two, you learn through pain." Subsequently Bad Dog shifted into other shapes: A soused teacher of seventh-grade civics. A football coach. A Professor of Male Pattern Baldness—the one who rubbed against his female students' legs, panting sherry and baring his teeth. Bad teacher! Down! Get in your house!

3. Lizard

Oh I, age seventeen, was hammering boulders at a gravel pit when Lizard took me to school. "I note," he rasped, "that everything originates with Sun, including what you call knowledge." At quitting time he added, "All creatures learn best by absorption. Relax, observe, bend. Be curious and still." Having sweated for wages, I was not amused. "But you are cold-blooded," I observed, arguing ad reptilium. "Hence," said Lizard, "my passion for Sun's instruction. You warm-blooded ones are ambitious and busy. You turn boulders into gravel. But you tend not to do well on the quizzes that count."

4. Squirrel

Later, when Seriousness befell me, I encountered Squirrel, a nervous careerist and tough grader. "Work," he advised, "scurry!

Perfect debating tricks, hoard grants, dress in gray, crack the whip of erudition. Heed my words and one day you shall oversee a knothole, perhaps rise to be a chancellor of nuts." Off, off I scrambled, my cheeks bursting with clever things to say.

5. Deer

Learned Deer, she of the polished obsidian hooves, stopped me in a meadow. Sky shone in her wide eyes. "The most dependable trails in Forest are intuitively mapped," she advised. "But I've established several goals with regard to what I seek," I said. "Excellent," said she. "For they will be here when you return with what you found you needed to learn. Whose woods these are, we only think we know."

6. Raccoon

One evening I was fortunate enough to hear Raccoon's keynote address to assembled pedagogical frogs:

"What I have learned from you, my friends," said Professor R, "is that good teachers are adaptable, must learn to move among states solid, fluid, and neither/nor." He continued: "I have learned that they must listen, as you listen with your eyes and ears and skin to sounds that strum your marsh. From auditing your evening classes, I have learned to appreciate a certain instructional jazz, the ad-hoc choral improv of your voicings, which at once are wholly serious and off-beat. From myself, a scholar in Night's archives, I have learned that knowing is an unfolding of illusions, as when I place a curious hand on a shining idea, only to see its factitude shimmer and disappear, to be replaced by some other image, intuition, text, or implication. Whether I return to dawn's bed hungry or sated, I am in either case informed." He paused, looking out over the pond, dotted with frogs' heads and decorated briefly with circles widening out from reeds. Raccoon went on: "As long as we know what we do not know, may we all briefly don the robe of confidence, play at authority. Dear frogs, fellow pedagogues, constant pupils of Mystery's moist matrices, I wish you continued curiosity, salute your evening evanescence!" Croaks of thanks rose from the water.

In praise and fascination, I thumped my large dry hands together, applauding Raccoon's remarks. The frogs shut up, swam deep. Raccoon glanced over his shoulder, rustled brush, disappeared. I was left to a lunar tutorial.

7. Snake

Snake was rumored to be one of the best teachers in those parts. She held a post at Tree of Knowledge State University. Her students brought her apples and compact discs. "What's the secret to teaching well?" I asked her. She grinned (then again, she grinned perpetually) and said, "Well, there's more than one, of course. But I would say that teachers should always remember themselves as students. We don't teach courses, ideas, ideals, or 'material.' The subject is students.—Oh, I might add—though of course I'm biased—that it helps to stay grounded."

Finis

Comma Splice
WILLIAM M. RAMSEY

For farmers it is a wall heaved down
and needing repair, to separate harvests
of hay from apple, home from intruder.

For those on death row it is a sentence
never finished, breath never stilled,
the heart never gassed to a dead stop.

For students it's a passing thought left
unresolved, abandoned for a new
beginning, a now without a past.

For commuters it is rushing to the
future, bumper to bumper,
despair and futility honked in transit.

For humanity, it's as if nothing ever comes
to full flower. All is in the bud.
Your most solemn word is cancelled by

the next desire or whim or chance.
Your universe expands ever onward,
neither true nor magnetic north

extending far with potent force.
A shaped thought is never thought,
a start stops a hope never finished.

The Grammarian

DARRELL G.H. SCHRAMM

> "Is wind a noun or a verb?"
> Naomi Shihab Nye, "Defining White"

The grammarian would say it's a noun,
always so sure of things:
Grammar hones the mind,
polishes reading skills,
anoints writing. And . . .

> *There's no research to prove that.*

. . . and wind is a noun that stays
in one place. And life
is an exorcise of wrong, an exercise
of right. The fork lies
on the left. Never gaze
at clouds. A field needs a fence.

> *With every word in place*
> *where is the space for language*
> *of vision?*
> *What happened years ago*
> *to him when the spirit moved*
> *across the face of the waters?*

What happened was this: It was autumn.
The rivers trembled. Ponds
denied the looking glass.
The grammarian held his breath,
would not let go
and refused to look at deciduous trees.

The Trouble with Writing

SARAH SLOANE

for William Stafford

A goat ate my pen. Frost grew
all over my computer
like a mossy beard and my keyboard fell
into a frozen stream, skidding towards a joke.
I forgot my notebook.
I don't have anything to say.

Meaning is always a half-
frozen thing,
thin sheets of ice floating
over winter water black as ink.

I don't know what to think
about this room full of twenty-year-olds writing
on the brink of the rest of their lives.

You are listening to me writing—
You who have forgotten your notebooks
You who like writing in invisible ink
You who believe that language cannot be owned
and copy out others' words
You who own a goat but no pen
You whose closest neighbor is Fear
You with the computer on the fritz
and the sixty-hour-a-week job at Costco
so you can afford to go here
You at the back
wondering what on earth
you might have to say—

Someone in the next room runs water.
I know you so well
the trouble with writing
is its own half-wit lying
under the sound
of each sound.

The Five Paragraph Essay

LEONORA SMITH

A five paragraph essay
reminds me of a blind date
with an ex-seminarian—
that long opening paragraph
of boring foreplay,
then the thesis: one, sterile,
over-emphatic thrust

not . . . awful, just . . . wearying.
And it goes on
with its three, dull interminable reasons
why I should take off my clothes,
each with its own turgid point:
he bought me steak, God said so,
we might die young.
His right hand, with its chilly fingers
trying to snake up my skirt,
the left fumbling—inept, but unrelenting—
trying to unhook my brassiere,
the strange medicinal smell
of his hard lipped kisses.

Each topic sentence with its own—
not very persuasive—support:
whispers that I'd love it,
grow huge breasts, be cured
of acne (I guess his scent—it's Clearasil).

Until, desperate,
approaching my curfew
or the end of the assigned 250 words,
he protrudes what he feels to be
his strongest argument into my ear
with his tongue—if I don't "do it"
his "things" will turn blue.

The Five Paragraph Essay

Not one real reason,
not one thing to remind me
why it's called "the body."

Then, the windows all fogged up,
and me wanting anything but this—
to read the comics, chew gum, nap—
we have to do the whole first part
all over again
because it's required that you have a conclusion—
a sad replay I am already forgetting
as the naugahyde scree-screes
under my garters
as I stare at the movement of my own shadow
in the foggy glass:

nothing worth remembering
nothing written here
worth taking home from school.

Scenes from the "Teaching Moment" Lounge

LYNNA WILLIAMS

Among the fiction writers in my graduate writing program, there were two absolutely-guaranteed-to-get-a-laugh punch lines. The first was the tag to an ancient dirty joke, "First you must @#$% him. Then you must give him a dollar." Its origin, not surprisingly, was a late night session at the Wagon Wheel Bar. The second was, "Oh, look. It's a teachable moment!" That line, of course, came from our "Teaching of Writing" class. Among the faculty who wandered in and out, it was simply a given that we would have these moments in our teaching lives. Epiphanies. Road-to-Damascus flashes of understanding. Lights coming on, flamenco dancers, ducks dropping from the ceiling: all of it. The only problem—and the reason we all thought the line was funny—was that every story we heard about a Teachable Moment seemed to involve a disaster of some kind in the classroom. Students who made out in the back row were a teachable moment, and students who thought grammar was a bourgeois plot were a teachable moment, and teachers who taught the hell out of Raymond Carver's "Fever" for 50 minutes—when the class had read Carver's "Feathers"—well, that was a teachable moment, too. After a while, none of us wanted to be anywhere near a T.M., unless we were also holding an airline ticket to Buenos Aires and the offer of a job from a Fortune 500 Company. What didn't occur to us at the time was the fundamental truth behind the stories: that, when things go terribly wrong, somebody might as well learn something.

Three months after I finished grad school, I was teaching my first (and ten years later, still my only) comp class at the university where I'm now an associate professor. Six weeks into the class, all was going well, I decided. Students who yawned covered their mouths, I got some points for being Southern in a classroom of kids from New Yawk and New Jersey, and every now and then I made a point or two about writing. At least I thought I had. But then we hit mid-term and the research paper. We talked about thesis statements and or-

Scenes from the "Teaching Moment" Lounge 143

ganization and library visits. We talked some more. On the day when the draft thesis statements were due, I went back to my office to look over them. In the middle of the pile, neatly centered on the page, was this thesis statement: "Technology is destroying man."

Okay, I thought, don't panic. I looked at the name on the paper; it belonged to a sweet, fast-talking boy from upstate New York, who told the class the first day he wanted to be "my generation's Sylvester Stallone."

The next day, when I began conferencing with class members about their thesis statements, Andy and I went into the corner to talk.

"It's an interesting premise," I said. "But do you think you could narrow it down a little?" I asked.

He asked me what I meant.

I told him. He asked me again. I told him. He asked me again. It was "Who's on first?" without the laughs, and I was getting a little desperate. I had already asked him to tell me what kind of technology was destroying man, without any luck, and I started throwing out possibilities.

"Computers?" I asked. "Crock pots? Safety razors? Lasers? The designated hitter? What? What technology is destroying man?"

He smiled—this was a very sweet student—and told me no, none of that was what he had in mind.

I smelled a Teachable Moment, and I went to find some other student to talk to.

The next class, when revisions of their thesis statements were due, Andy's said, "Technology is destroying man."

Another conversation (different corner) followed. At the time it didn't occur to me to try listening to Andy, to try finding out what about that line was so compelling to him. I wanted it narrowed, or I wanted it gone.

And so I kept pushing. Finally, after four weeks and four sheets of "Technology is destroying man," I decided that if my mother could use Tough Love to get me to quit running with what was called, in my West Texas high school, "that rough philosophy crowd," I could use some Tough English.

Narrow it down, or else, I told him. He smiled, and went away.

The very next day, Andy showed up at my office hours bearing a piece of paper on his open palm, like a treasure.

"I did it," he said. "I thought about what you said, and I did it."

He handed me the paper, and I looked down at this thesis statement. "Technology is destroying man in Ohio."

I did not laugh out loud, although it was close. I talked to him about Ohio, about the canals and the rivers that no longer carry men and goods to their destinations, about the communities that once thrived and have now disappeared, about the festivals that are held for tourists now, not for people who make their lives on the water.

It was my first Teachable Moment, and my favorite still.

PART FIVE

Memories of Our Children and Families Learning

Beast on the Brink

JANE BARNES

When you are sitting across from me reading
from the latest copy of *Time*
or silently devouring the pages
of that history you love so much,
I wonder how we will talk when
words are unavailable.
You are so devoted
to ideas and I,
I feel the categories of logic
ebbing from my brain,
ideas scrambling behind them like stones,
a scree, no longer scrutable.
Soon I will be chattering or howling
on this inchoate, imaginary shore
and maybe you
will look up from your book and wonder
who this creature is
who came in and took me
out of my comfortable chair
while you were reading.

Geography Lessons

GRACE BAUER

What's Nebraska? asks Adam,
who is eight and curious
about why I have left the familiar
state we both lived in since
the year he was born. Too wide-eyed
for irony, he studies my face
for an answer, a definition of this
marvelous word I now abide in
but can't yet explain. So I mumble
It's flat and far away, trying
to sum up the difference between
now and the four hours of Blue Ridge
we once drove across to visit.

If I had a map, I'd point
almost dead-center, as if abstractions
like that would satisfy a child,
even one who understands directions
a damn sight better than I do,
with my endless circling
of back roads and main streets
trying to find my way back
to places I've just recently been.

He knows distance, I'm sure,
and something about longing—
one of the first lessons anyone learns.
But how do I describe the absence here,
that so many fall in love with?
Which words will allow him to picture
the predominance of sky? I take his *what*
at face value, an honest inquiry
into more than location, and struggle
with the wide space in the language
I am still trying to imagine into place.

Everything We Need

DEVAN COOK

A few days after Christmas I was at my parents' house, standing in the bathroom—door open, light on—braiding my hair to pin it up while I showered. Like Mom's, my hair is gray, coarse, and dry: it doesn't benefit from daily washing.

Mom was pacing, as she often did after breakfast, from one end of the house to the other. "Do you have everything you need?" she asked. I don't think she knew who I was: this was one of her set speeches, elaborately-constructed stratagems that allow her to function socially—to be involved and to act—even when she doesn't know where she is, whom she is with, or who she is.

Asking whether I have everything I need implies that she could, in fact, provide it. She's asked the question hundreds of times as her Alzheimer's disease progresses. I like the way she stakes out her territory, even now. Dad dumped Miss Alabama for this woman, now tiny and white-haired, her eyes as opaque as a stuffed wren's. What choice did he have? She wanted him.

Usually my sister or brother or I tell her that we need a hug, thanks, and she hugs us enthusiastically, or with reservations if she doesn't know us. This time I was hot and sweaty from working out, eager to wash.

"Yes, Mom, I'm fine," I said.

She seemed disappointed, so I went on. "I'm Devan. I'm an English professor at Boise State University, and I came to see you for Christmas, and I'm going to be here for a few more days."

She looked at me. "You're visiting from Idaho? You're a teacher? A professor? You are?"

"Yes, Mom. I'm Professor Cook, Dr. Devan Cook, thanks to you and Dad." She clasped my hands; she beamed.

"Say it again," she said. "Say it. Say it."

i'm very proud of her

GERALD LOCKLIN

i am deeply touched when,
at the hotel where i am staying
on academic business,
i observe the young couples,
gangly and serious as young bucks and fawns,
filing from cloakroom to ballroom
for their senior prom.

in two weeks my beloved daughter
will be going to hers.

she's always had an active social life,
but she definitely preferred
the counterculture coffeehouses
to the formal dances.

a week ago, though, when i was
talking her into taking an advanced
    placement test
about which she had some severe
    apprehensions,
telling her that it was important that we learn
to override our fears of failure,
to prove ourselves,
not to others,
but to ourselves,

she said, "in other words,
i should take the exam
for the same reason that
i'm going to my senior prom."

"i didn't know," i said, "that that
was why you were going, but yes,

i'm very proud of her

you're right, it's breaking through a barrier
that seems more solid than it is."

the next morning she went off to take the test
and never mentioned it again.
the results have not arrived yet,
but as far as i'm concerned,
she's passed already
in a blaze of glory.

Academic Kids

Janet McCann

Your father asks you, how many
Hairs make a beard? I send you
From the room so I can describe you,
Promising later we'll make a
Perpetual motion machine. Your
Eyes grow round from trying to
Understand, even the two-year-old
Needs glasses. You puzzle patiently
Over things, trying to keep up, even
To add, but then at night
In muttering sleep I glean your
Planned rebellions: you will
Get married at sixteen.
You will be hunters, you will drive
Garbage trucks. You will run over
Paper, pages, words, stamp on them,
Kick them to bits. Your children
Will run naked through the woods, their
Bodies fitting them like light,
And never write our names.

Can You Predict the Past?
Can You Remember the Future?

Janet McCann

my son tells me Hitler was elected
by one vote, he learned this in school,
with other times a vote
derailed history. I am skeptical,

he learns a lot of lies in school
many from teachers. his voice climbs up
over the tv, he is excited.
history is cool, he says, I wish

I could've been there, to vote against
Hitler. I think, it's what they tell you
to make you want to vote. I want him
to want to vote, so I say nothing.

besides, it might be true. one vote, he says,
and Texas would be outside the Union. one
vote and we'd all be speaking German.
I wish I could've been there.

Becky's Mirror

DEAN NEWMAN

I know I had on those heavy, steel-toed boots—my legs felt like lead on each step up to the front porch of the house. I must have been working with logs—cutting lodge pole pines—peeling them with a drawknife—laying them out—notching them—rolling them up an incline with a kant hook—bone tired. So it must have been '79 or '80, and my legs were lead, and I sat on the top step and began to unlace the boots and struggle them off my tired feet.

Then I heard my daughter's voice behind me—Leah—two or three then. Probably three. When I turned around and looked, I could see her through the sliding glass door—sitting on the floor and talking to herself. It was that adult, mother voice she used with her dolls.

Watching a child play when they don't know you're watching is better than stopping to smell any roses I've ever smelled. It's a sweet, sweet, painful moment because we're grown up, and we know.

In my stockinged feet, carrying my heavy boots, I moved slowly toward the door so I could see her better without catching her attention.

She sat splay-legged on the floor with a doll sitting between her legs. Leah was brushing Becky's hair. Becky had on a brown, gingham dress—but no shoes—eaten by the dog. Becky's hat, a wide brimmed sun hat with a ribbon hanging down the back, lay on the floor beside her. Leah was telling her what pretty hair she had. She told Becky more sternly, "Try to stay clean for ten minutes and don't wipe your nose on your new dress."

Then she sensed me watching.

She leapt up and ran to the door with Becky tucked tightly under her arm, leaned hard against the glass to help me push the sliding door open, then threw her free arm around one of my legs and, now in her wounded child voice, said, "Dad, one of the boys took Becky's meer, and they won't tell me where it is." Jesse and Jeremy—her two older brothers.

At that moment—I don't know why—I decided I should correct my daughter's pronunciation. I said, "Honey, it's mir-ror—the word is mir-ror."

I don't know what I expected from such a little girl, but when she stopped hugging my leg and looked up at me—without speaking—looking me in the eyes—gauging something, I think—I felt doubt and said, "It's pronounced mir-ror."

Leah's mouth opened slightly—in a look that I swear was grown up doubt. With a bit of a sneer, she said, "No it's not."

Feeling very sure of myself about this, I said "Yes it is. It's mir-ror."

She sighed a deep, bothered sigh and took me by my free hand and led me, still carrying the heavy boots, across the living room and down the hall to the bathroom. She pulled me inside and shut the door behind us. She stepped up to the full length mirror on the back of the door—looked at her reflection for a moment—a long moment—then she looked up at me and said, "See that, Dad? That's me. It's a Me-er."

Brains and Books

DIANE PAYNE

Walking back home, daypack filled with books, I see Grandpa sitting on his porch swing, and cross the street to join him.

"Whatdya have in that heavy bag?" he asks.

"Books."

"Don't be wasting your hard-earned money on books!"

"I didn't buy them, Grandpa. I was at the library," I say, quietly regretting I didn't own them.

"You're never gonna get a husband if you keep reading all those books. If you smile nice at the restaurant, a nice boy will ask you on a date. But, if he finds out about those books, he won't date you."

"Oh, Grandpa! It's not like that anymore. Only families go to the restaurant, and old people. Boys don't hang out at Veurink's Kitchen. And it doesn't matter how much I smile at those customers, they don't tip anyways."

"Oh, they pay enough to eat there. They shouldn't have to tip."

"Want to play Aggravation?" I say. Grandpa made the game board himself, and I think it's just the game we need right now.

We go inside his apartment and he hauls out the heavy board. Grandma is cleaning houses today. Even though neither of them reads, Grandma would have rolled her eyes so Grandpa couldn't have seen her, if she heard Grandpa make that comment about books and boys. The only book in their home is the Bible, and it's written in Dutch.

We say nothing while we play the game. Grandpa prefers it to be quiet, but he doesn't really like to be alone.

"You won't get a husband if you keep reading those books," he says after we've been playing quietly for ten minutes, not letting this warning go unheard.

"What am I going to do in college if I don't read books?"

"You ain't going to college. Girls don't need all that fancy schooling. Your dad can get you a good job at the factory. That's where you'll meet a good husband."

I start conjuring up images of the men I'll meet who are like my dad, and this makes me more determined never to work at GM. "I don't want to work at a factory or waitress all my life. I want to be a teacher or a writer. I need to go to college."

"I win," he says ignoring me, sounding like Eeyore from the Pooh books.

Grandpa starts picking up the game, his way of saying it's time to go.

Walking past the five houses between our homes, I wave and shout greetings to the neighbors sitting on their steps, feeling the books pound against my back, as I wonder how I'll ever make it into college, deciding that even if I don't get to go, I'll keep reading. Looking at all the houses on our block, I realize how few contain a bookshelf, how few people have even graduated from high school, but somehow I know I'll live in a house with bookshelves, and I'll still be playing Aggravation with Grandpa.

Fish, Spring, Window

LEONORA SMITH

> "If I could look at him long enough, I should see his dreams."
> Ouspensky, "In Search of the Miraculous"
> in Colin Wilson's *The Occult*

These students, dopey with spring—their heads
bob over the text like droopy mums.
Behind their wavering eyelids, there's more to see—

as glancing out your window you might glimpse
a cloud of sparrows flitting between trees, or even a veldt
where zebras prance in tall grass, instead of Cincinnati—

something real or imagined snatching your attention
like the moment when you are not exactly first in love
but just after that, when you suddenly can't believe your luck,

or like the moment I woke up after my son was born, his head
pointy from forceps—no matter how flat his forehead was,
he was so beautiful. Or my husband watching the fish

dart and flash in his aquarium—the African Cichlids who
    evolved
their own near-marine colors sequestered in the rift lakes
Tanganyika and Malawi, an underwater Galapagos.

He overcrowds them, so there's no room
for territoriality. Still they bump one another with their snouts
when they cross paths, who is big enough

to eat whom mapping the space they take, a paisley
of motion, a pattern you can almost see—if you know it's
    there—
in the near-invisible water. The way I see bits of my students'
    dreams

as bright flashings over their bored-looking heads—
all of us improbably jammed together in this room against
 nature—
like flickers of tiny Northern lights, in cardinal,

gold and turquoise—a Red Empress, a Peacock, an Electric
Blue—run-amuck auras, some more than a little cannibal,
but all shimmery as aquarium fish, or the rainbow halos of
 circus angels.

A Rhetoric of Wood

MICHAEL SPOONER

"Word is present in each and every act of understanding."
Mikhail Bakhtin

In February, just-five, and master
of the shoelace, Isaac ties
on a canvas apron. "Can I borrow
your hammer? Mine's dirty."

I remember my father's tools,
his father's name on them,
acid-etched in crabbed script.
How dense and heavy
their metal parts were,
how smooth their wooden handles
from generations of hands.

"Where's my saw—the one with the handle
like a question? This garage is cold.
If we spill just a little kerosene,
the house will only be a little bit on fire."

Take a look at this, I say.
*See the waves and lines of color
in the wood? That's "grain."*

"Grain," Isaac ponders, testing the word.
And "I have a question," he says.
"Why are these sand bags in the truck?
Watch me jump from one to th'other."

The trouble is that some knowledge
passes only hand to hand.
My father's reverence for wood
never came to me until I,

like Isaac now, bit pine
with my own blade, until
I raised a fingerful of new
sawdust to my tongue
or rubbed a finish smooth
with my own hand.

Isaac, just-February-five, and
master of the I-Can-Read,
hammers one more nail
poof into the drywall, and puts away
his question-mark saw.

"Grain," I hear him mutter,
and I almost think Bakhtin was right.
"But what would happen," Isaac asks himself,
"if we poured every grain
of sand out of these bags?"

X
Doyle Wesley Walls

My son only wants to type the "x" on the screen.
He holds his finger down:
xxxxxxxxxxxxxxxxxxxxxxxxxxxxxxxxxxxxxxxxxxxxxxxx.
I'm tired, overworked, and now angry with him.
"No," I say. "Either write something
or stop wasting my time."

He's disappointed. In time, he types,
"i ws lukng at the stars last niht."

I leave, return. He's gone back to
xxxxxxxxxxxxxxxxxxxxxxxxxxxxxxxxxxxxxxxxxxxxxxxx.
Perhaps it's something
that has to be said, something
he can never finish writing,
each "x" one time
when our paths crossed.

What thunder I roared tonight,
what a scene when he ate
without closing his mouth,
without eating over his plate!
He waves the tines of his fork
near his eyes and
interrupts when my wife or I talk!
Yesterday on his trike
he almost ran over
the two-year-old Sarah!

He's five. How many times
must I repeat myself?
Be kind! Be careful! Think!

In 5th grade Jon suggested
we slam the door on Annette,

who was to hold the door for us all,
as we walked past her into class.
The two boys in front of me did, and
the third time is automatic.
I didn't think she'd be hurt.
I didn't think.
Mrs. Muldrew, livid, singled me out,
made me look up at her, said
she expected more from me than that.

Seth's asleep. I'm walking
under stars. I stop and force myself
to look up.
I always thought I'd be
a stellar daddy.
Go on, stupid, I think to myself,
*you know who you are, write your name,
write your name, stupid.*

With the heel of my shoe
I make my "x" in the sandbox. I fill
the box with "x" after "x" for the many
times I have been cross with him here
on the playground.

It is so far from this sandbox to
the stars. The way they shine.

Roses and Tulips

Jane Elkington Wohl

    for Melinda

It is all so ordinary:
the men installing the new furnace,
the broken spring on the storm door,
(they must hold it open while they struggle
the bulky box strapped to the dolly over the threshold).
One of them comes into the living room
to tell us that the water will be off for an hour.

The air begins to chill
and you pull your coat over your knees
as we discuss Faulkner—;
your English paper,
Emily's decaying life,
a desiccated, long-dead rose.
This is a paper I have assigned, read, re-read,
written a hundred times, and yet,
today I am not the teacher
and I listen as you struggle,
annotate, underline, re-word,
until finally, you begin to tell me
that you are divorcing,
that you have no money,
that your red-haired son flies
comet-like across your day,
freed now from his father's harping on his faults,
that your daughter came in last night
and talked and talked in ways she never had before,
"I just want to be his friend, Mama," she says,
more afraid of hurting than of being hurt.
You wish you could tell her friendship is possible
and think maybe it is for her.

Roses and Tulips

The house grows colder.
I begin to wish I'd put on a sweater,
the tip of my nose begins to chill
even on this mild February day.
The tulips you have brought me
flame on the end table
as you tell me how little you have to spend for food.
What is Faulkner in the face of courage?
On the phone you said you had so much to say
but you didn't have the tools,
the ways of putting grief on paper.
Now I lend you a book on how to write,
how to translate thought to words,
as if with words we can each define our lives,
tell stories of elusive pasts,
let words, like tulips, flame against decay.

And I think of that man from Mississippi,
writing of death, of dreams
and finally, what in our ordinary lives,
we might call love.

Part Six

Remembering Those Who Taught Us

A Note About Allen Tate

Kelly Cherry

I took Literary Criticism with Allen Tate. My mind was not on the subject, because—I liked to think—I preferred the abstractions of philosophy and the music of poetry to the explication of the obvious. Literary criticism seemed to me to be mostly paraphrase. But I have since learned to love writing about writing, and perhaps the real reason I was distracted, that bright autumn semester so long ago, was that I had fallen in love. I was going to be married over the Christmas break.

Mr. Tate—we called him "Mr." Tate, not "Dr." or "Professor," and never in our wildest dreams "Allen"—began each class by reading the roll. *Present*, I would say, staring out the window and thinking about licenses, announcements, what dress to wear. *Here*. I wasn't, really.

While he went down the list of last names, Mr. Tate played with his cigarette lighter. It was, I'm sure, a gold lighter. It *looked* gold, and I doubt that Mr. Tate would ever have been happy with something that looked gold but was not gold. He flipped the lid open. Twirled, with his thumb, the little wheel that ignited the wick. The lighter flared. He snapped the lid shut. Sometimes he snapped the lid shut with the thumb of the same hand with which he was holding the lighter; sometimes he gently palmed the lid shut with his other hand.

Oddly, I can't remember whether he smoked in class. It's likely that he did; I think that teachers probably were allowed to smoke in class in those days. But in those days everyone I knew smoked. But not everyone I knew—in fact, no one else I knew—had a gold cigarette lighter. It was the lighter, not the smoking, that was interesting. The lighter, and that Mr. Tate played with it nervously all through class.

He was slender, shortish, with a formal bearing. His manners were of a kind seldom encountered today: the enactment of established rituals of courtesy and consideration. To shake his hand was to participate in a small ceremony. To pass him in the hallway and say hi was to play a minor but, one understood, important part in a well-known drama. (And never a melodrama.)

Maybe there were melodramas in his life. I wouldn't know, because I didn't know him outside of class. He was not the kind of teacher a shy student got to know outside the classroom. Maybe *he* was shy. He certainly did fiddle nervously with that cigarette lighter.

He addressed us with a title, too. We were "Mr." or "Miss." (I have to interrupt myself here to say that although "Ms." had, according to the Oxford English Dictionary, been invented, it had not yet arrived in North Carolina, so he can hardly be faulted for not using it.)

Jonathan Silver and I were married at my parents' house in front of a picture window while the worst blizzard in Richmond's history whited out the view. Guests gazed forlornly at their cars being buried under drifts of snow. Jonathan's mother and father had refused to attend; the mood was solemn, more suited to political and religious history than to romance. There was a sense that we were all engaged in a subversive activity, but against our will, as if we were also surprised, and unsettled, to discover ourselves engaging in anything subversive. People wanted to be in their own homes, not facing the prospect of digging out, putting on snow chains, driving down unplowed roads. As soon as the minister pronounced us husband and wife, coats were grabbed, and people stood in the foyer, sweating in swathes of scarves, waiting only for Jonathan and me to leave first. We had borrowed my father's car. As we turned the corner, I looked back to see the party, which had never quite begun, breaking up. The picture window framed the scene, and it was like something by Hopper, beautiful and sad.

There were two weeks remaining in the semester after the holidays. The first day I returned to Literary Criticism, Mr. Tate, as usual, called the roll, but he did not read my name among the Cs. He read most of the roll without stopping. When he reached the *S*s, he stopped to flick his gold lighter open. Then he called, "Mrs. Silver."

Here, I answered. *Present.*

He flicked his lighter shut and finished the roll call.

That was all. But I knew that this man—this deeply quiet man—had paid more attention to me than I ever had paid to Literary Criticism. Perhaps contemporary women, who prefer "Ms." to "Mrs." and who keep their own names instead of changing them, won't like this story. But I am a contemporary woman, who has reclaimed her own name, and yet I remember the day Mr. Tate called me by my married name as the day I learned what literary criticism is all about. Literary criticism is about the interlineation of text and interpretation. It is about locating new meaning in the words we have been given. It is about knowing how to call the roll—with respect, that is, and observantly, in a way that recognizes change in the world.

To an Ex-Student,
On Learning She Is a World-Class Gymnast

STEPHEN COREY

    for Ann Woods

What routines you must have mounted
in Mycenae and Greece
while the rest of us studied texts
in our windowless room:
Your chalked palms know
they can vault the Cretan bull's horns,
your spine curling down
to the rough, frothing beam of his back.
In the Test of the Bow, you dance
across the axe-halves, beggaring
even the hero's threaded shot.
You sit with a hand on Homer's thigh
as that night's *Odyssey* becomes itself.
As the poet fights
the strange and familiar magic of his brain,
your touch reminds him
the tongue is first a muscle.
Your silent sprung flights and twistings show
what the body of his song can be.

Mr. Howard
Geraldine DeLuca

Mr. Howard was tall and skinny as a crane. He had a narrow pock-marked face, a large nose, pale eyes and brown hair. When he spoke to us, he stood against a chair and folded his leg in front of him. Always, he carried an unlit pipe, and every week he told us not to smoke. We all did—me and my girlfriends, Judy, Donna, Barbara and Mary Ann—and we never considered quitting. But we loved him for telling us we should.

We loved his ugly face, his skinny body, his bent leg on the chair and his unlit pipe. We loved that there was a sadness about him and thought it had to do with his ugliness and some illness caused by cigarettes. Maybe under his shirt he had a scar. We loved that in this school of *Silas Marner* and *Ethan Frome*, he taught creative writing. We loved that he let us write haiku all over the board, that he asked us to notice as the spring blossoms unfolded in the tree outside the window.

And who was I, apart from the we of the five of us, the "big five" we actually called ourselves? Alone, I didn't expect him to notice me. Judy and Donna were the really smart ones in English. Barbara was a dancer. Mary Ann was a genius at math. But who was I?

For our final project we had to find a short story and turn it into a radio play. I chose a story from *Seventeen* magazine about a young man who throws balls against the wall of an empty playground. I don't remember much about the story—just the sound of the ball being lobbed against the wall.

I sat in my bedroom in the new upholstered chair my parents bought as an offering to keep me there, and I lived inside the story of the lonely man. He had to talk to somebody, so I created a girl with shoulder-length brown hair. For awhile, the two of them understood each other. They didn't stay friends, but what they shared was important to them.

The play felt deep to me. I handed it in on the last day of class and never got it back. I never learned what he thought, and gradually I came to fear that I had offended him.

After high school, I cut my hair and moved out of my parents' home. I got a job and went to college in the city. Years later, in graduate school, I saw him standing in the hall waiting for a class to begin. It startled me to see him there, just a face in a group, waiting. I didn't speak to him. I didn't say he had been my teacher, that I'd loved writing the radio play for him. I didn't say I'd stopped smoking. I wanted to talk to him, but I was afraid. Maybe he wouldn't remember me. Or worse, maybe he would.

Mystery and Manners

Marvin Diogenes

"Dr. Kopkind?" I asked the man standing at the emergency room check-in.

"Dr. K?" He'd been my professor in a fiction writing class the previous fall; now, he was thinner than I remembered, the paunch gone, his face angular over a close-cropped goatee.

He turned and stared, slack-eyed, taking in my brown security guard's uniform. "Gordo?" He focused, attempted a smile. "Gordon Sievers, right? You were working on an alcoholic father story."

I nodded. I had that story in a folder in the guard shack, next to a pile of textbooks.

"Good start on that piece, as I recall," Dr. K said.

The woman he was standing with at the check-in glanced at me and then turned her attention back to the nurse. She held her right wrist in her left hand, gingerly, away from her chest. I could see how striking her features were, framed by shiny brackets of black hair. She wore dark glasses and a bulky slate gray sweater, though it was almost three A.M. on a warm June night.

"Rosalind Dasher," an aide called from the hallway leading to X-ray.

The woman started away from the desk. Dr. K stepped with her. She stopped and pulled her wrist to her breast.

"I'll be right here," he said.

"Yes. Stay here. I'll need a ride." When she reached the aide, she smiled and said, "Lead the way. I've always depended on the kindness of strangers."

Dr. K remembered I was there. "My wife, Gordo. That was my wife." He had not mentioned a wife when I was in his class. "My reason for being. My fate. You married, Gordo?"

"Soon, I hope." The stack of textbooks—Accounting, Finance, Business Administration—was my dowry, in a way. Finishing my degree was a condition Ellie had placed on marrying me. A degree in hand, and she would be mine. That was the deal.

"Then learn from this, Gordo, for future reference. Why are my wife and I here?"

"An emergency. Your wife hurt her wrist."

"How?"

I didn't figure him for a wife-beater. Though he talked in class about how we needed to explore all that our characters were capable of, he stressed even more the importance of the moral sense, the certainty that human beings mattered, could change, were capable of achieving grace.

"An accident," I said.

"No. She took a swing at me. I ducked. A reflex. She slammed the microwave instead of my jaw." He massaged his goatee. "I think her wrist is broken. Sprained, at least."

"Still an accident."

"No, Gordon. I promised I wouldn't duck. I promised I would accept the blows."

"Whoa," I said.

"Watch when she comes out of X-ray. Watch us together. Write what you see." He stretched his neck to look down the hall where his wife had gone.

"Help me with the mystery here. You've got time, right? Long nights standing guard at the emergency room."

I told him I had to make my hourly rounds—parking lot, outside doors, the lawns on which I sometimes caught local teenagers making out.

"Okay," he said. "I'm gonna wait for my wife." I moved toward the door.

"We don't sleep much," he said. "I can hardly get up for class." He raised his hand, splayed his fingers in my direction. "Maybe you can come by the office some time."

I left the emergency room and began to walk the hospital grounds. I walked quickly but checked everything I was supposed to. There was time before Dr. K's wife would finish in X-ray and consult with the doctor on duty. I would watch and do what Dr. K had asked. He'd been a good teacher, and he looked like he could use some help.

For W. H. Auden and Alain Bombard

SKIP EISIMINGER

One may survive
a wreck at sea
if one starts to drink
immediately
a pint of brine
per day for thirst
and a squirt of plankton
seined in a shirt.

I wanted to write this
that along the way
a poem may be said
to have saved the day.

Highlights

DOUGLAS GOETSCH

Drunk, her eyes would water and sparkle
and she'd hold my jaw in her palm
as though I were her child or dog, saying,
*Listen to me, Douglas. Don't dare turn
into one of these aging bachelor teachers.*
Then she'd reel off names of half a dozen
doddering men in the physics and social
studies departments who wandered the halls
in stained shirts and chalked-up pants
frayed at the pockets, men first in line
every day in the faculty cafeteria,
men who stared deadpan into the lens
of the yearbook photographer.

Come with me, she said. We took a cab
to her gay guy in the Village. She said
I needed once and for all a decent
haircut. She was first. Barry
put a tight rubber cap on her head
and used a hooked needle to pull
strands of her wet hair through holes
until she looked like a shock therapy patient,
her face pale and tired in the light,
and suddenly she was a woman
twenty years older than me getting
highlights. Though she looked damn
good when it was over, climbing
down from the chair in her red shoes.
We found a bar on Bleecker Street.
She put a hand through my new haircut
while I complained about the girls in American
Literature who were giving me problems.
She said they were in love with me,

and wondered at how blind I was
to miss it. Then she told me, finally,
where she went every weekend: Tampa,
to stay with an auto parts salesman
who paid her fare. A man her age, a man
who used to be married to her sister.

Long Overdue Note to My College Professor Who Broke Down and Cried One Morning in 1974 While Teaching Yeats

DAVID GRAHAM

At long last I know what you mean.
That was no country for any man,
that classroom with its fluorescent rows
of groggy juniors equal in fear

and indifference. We were in
no one's arms but yours, and you split
open like a shell to reveal
the raw jelly inside. We froze,

thinking it was family woe,
maybe an old back injury
acting up, perhaps even fear
of tenure's blank guillotine.

Maybe so, maybe so. Now I
think it was us, our practiced slouch,
our gaze blank and pitiless as
the clock itching toward hour's end.

We weren't about to love Yeats
on your say-so. We were thinking
grades, thinking lunch, thinking firelight
playing upon a girlfriend's skin,

and we were thinking them so hard
we couldn't feel what you said
Yeats felt. So in piteous rage
at our held breaths, our cautious nods,

Long Overdue Note

you wept. And we didn't know how
to be anything but polite
about it. You stammered, halted,
and stood bent over the lectern

in pain. We studied our notes. We
glanced at the swaying trees outside
while you cried silently into,
over, and about our silence.

Seminar

SHANNON MARQUEZ MCGUIRE

for Milton Rickels, Southwestern Louisiana University

But tonight, another crime, besides the way it
fought to carve your voice away,
the monstrous thing that killed you.
The dying of those evenings we all loved:
At home, you sat up in a high-backed leather chair,
ensconced before we showed our faces at your door.
You spread the books you loved across
the fat-legged, polished table at your side,
then waved us in, called out each name,
adding in *It's Old So-and-so* or *Kiddo*.

You bid us find a rocker and help ourselves to wine.
We pulled our circle closer to your chair.
We tasted roasted peanuts scooped from a copper bowl,
and sipped at amber sherry from the glasses in our hands
as if its nutty burning was an old, familiar flavor,
licked salt from tips of fingers and chatted till you'd start.
You fed us Twain or Frost; you asked us
quiet questions, so simple on the surface,
then listened, really listened, to what we said.

And partway through the night, you made us rest
and let us wander through your book-lined, windowed den,
and over to a dining room where coffee steamed and waited.
We toasted hands and faces at a fire you had stoked.
Against the wall, a buffet and a platter piled with pears.
(Your wife whispered how you dearly loved to see them.)
beneath a simply framed and simply painted scene:
laundry dancing on a line, some dark-skinned children
playing under trees whose shade they'd never need to leave.

Seminar

Then, taking up our books, we got to rocking.
You sat with us around you, lamplight shining your pages,
your crutches tucked into the shadows, no need this night
for help to make your way. No guru from some mount,
you hated pretense, so we listened to a man and watched
your gnarled but gentle hands, and learned your secrets:

Marrow's strength in falsely fragile bones.
California wines from boyhood hillsides.
Vermilion River's entrenched, muddy way.
Cayenned catfish stews, roux-darkened gumbos.
Woman's tenderness and losing's pain.
Fury at wrong, no matter whose and every time.
Lust for every joke that binds us to this earth.
The power of the word kept on the page.
Teaching's rapture shining from your eyes.

The Physics Teacher

ANNE-MARIE OOMEN

    for Norm Wheeler

He wanted to believe something defied the laws.

The day the hawk slammed
into the big cathedral windows
and dropped like a stone,
he was teaching Newton,
trying to make it easy:

Something moving wants to keep moving,
something at rest wants to stay that way.

He leads the class outside.
Great bird, not dead but still,
one eye blurred,
he sets in a box, closes the top,
puts it in the principal's office.

After the second law:
Force equals mass times acceleration.
Okay, take it like this—
the faster you go and bigger you are,
the more force you create—
he has to go back, thinking
how heavy, massive the bird.

Physics students, the bright, skeptical ones
follow and when he lifts
the flap of cardboard,
they barely see the bird burst
like fire toward the white wall,
oceanscape, window light.
In the corner, his gloved hands close

on its mad flutter, caping the beak,
muting the scream.

The third law:
for every action there is an equal
and opposite reaction.

He holds out the bird like an offering,
stares back into the fierce, opaque eye.
Passing the secretary's window
the thrum between his palms
pushes so strongly his hands could break.

He croons *Not yet, not yet*
then shouts to the physics kids
Outside! We've got to get it outside.

The thing, awake, straining and wild,
knows the light, fights his grip.

Is there another law?

He rushes down the sterile hall,
arms locked—

The doors! Open the doors!

A dozen hands pull wide the double winter doors.
He does not feel the talons pierce his wrist,
or the opposing force of wings in his face.
His own hands open and the bird
explodes into its own law and beauty.

Sister Albert

BILL RANSOM

Sixty-two students crowded the room right up to Sister Albert's desk, and her chair snugged against the blackboard.

"You said you weren't coming back this year." Her white wimple bobbed under her chin. She waved a chalky hand at my gawking ex-classmates. "Where would we put you?" With a nod, she indicated her typewriter. "On that?"

My humiliation thickened the air.

Besides teaching seventh and eighth grade, she was the principal, which got her a typewriter on a stand beside her desk. The giggling stopped at a lift of her eyebrow.

"You got in a fight and got kicked out your first day in public school," she said. "So now we all have a black eye. What should we do about that?"

"I don't know," I said, and shrugged. I just wanted to disappear.

Sister mumbled something, then told me to take the typewriter out and bring in a desk. "And try not to block the doorway."

Twice a day I made a path to the door and swapped my desk for Sister's typewriter stand. I cleaned the boards and the erasers, emptied the wastebaskets and straightened desks every afternoon while Sister finished her work. Two weeks into the term, she entered me into a regional speech contest.

"But, Sister," I said, "I can't even talk in front of class."

"Then let's start slow," she said. "For the rest of the week, I'll work in the hallway after school while you practice in here alone. Next week I'll work in here while you practice. The week after, neither of us will work while I listen to you practice. The contest is that Saturday. It's a cinch; here's your speech."

I knew the speech cold the first day, but I thought she'd let me off the hook if I couldn't get it right—like the time I threw the fifth grade spelling bee. Sister didn't seem concerned, so that last day I asked to drop out.

"Whether you win or not," she said, "it'll be a good experience."

Suddenly, I hated her.

"I won't do it." I was breathing like I'd been running, and my fists were clenched.

Sister stood up and stepped up so close that I could smell the coffee on her breath. She blinked once, planted her feet and said, "You want to hit me?"

I wanted to hit somebody.

"If you want to hit me, then hit me," she said.

I saw that I was taller.

"Do you want to hit me?"

She was the only adult in a month who'd spent time with me.

"No, Sister," I said, and dropped my hands. "I just want to go home."

"Then do it once more, just for fun, and we can both go home."

All Hail Digredi

Angus Woodward

According to legend, most students signed up for Dr. Digredi's *Intro 101* accidentally, not knowing for sure what the course title meant or whether it had any application to their undeclared majors, so that it was rare for there to be more than ten students in his classes, although those that survived the course tended to become lifelong friends. The experience cemented them, the same way passengers on flights in which the pilot, copilot, and navigator suffer heart attacks and a recently divorced stewardess must be talked through landing the jet in a thunderstorm which threatens the lives of her children in a far-off houseboat tend to feel a deep, life-long affinity.

The foundation for his students' attachment to Dr. Digredi and each other was laid in the first class session, which began with Dr. Digredi holding up copies of the syllabus, although he typically strayed momentarily to inform the students that *syllabus* came from a Greek word meaning *parchment strip used as a label*, which inevitably led him to offer a brief cultural history of writing surfaces from stone to mylar, at which point he could hardly resist detailing the ebb and flow of technological development and its influence on human affairs and expression, although he seemed to have hardly begun describing nineteenth century computers when the glimmering field of mathematics beckoned him and he plunged into a wondrous exposition of number theory. Halfway through congruence, Dr. Digredi paused, took a deep breath, and posed a question: "What are we to make of the fact that many primitive cultures have flood myths predating their contact with 'civilized' Europeans?" A young man in the second row might shift in his chair, begin to lift an arm, but Digredi would be off again, weaving a brilliant rhapsody on the power of narrative, managing at one point to touch on *The Iliad* and the Simpson trial in the same breath, the latter helping him to make a smooth transition into an impromptu treatise on the future of jurisprudence and the potential dangers of online cross examination.

Soon, explications of the global economy, the Coriolis effect, helicopter mechanics, the Korean War, the Pinyin system, orthography, the Gutenberg Bible, predestination, positivism, Alessandro Volta, and electronic music spiraled out of Dr. Digredi's mouth in dizzying succession.

At this point Dr. Digredi paused, wiped his brow with a vermilion bandanna, and glanced at his watch. "All right," he sighed. "I suppose that will be enough for now." He began to gather his belongings from the podium, but invariably one of the dazed students raised her hand.

"Anything we should do for next time, Dr. Digredi?"

Here Dr. Digredi fixed the class with a kind smile. "There is no 'next time.' Perhaps you did not notice the sun rising and setting as I spoke, or the leaves falling and snow drifting. The semester is over. Enough said."

Groggy and hungry, the class staggered out behind Dr. Digredi. They dispersed and found the way home, where their loved ones hardly recognized them.

Afterword: The Art of Pedagogy/ The Pedagogy of Art

DAVID STARKEY

The Art of Pedagogy

It starts, perhaps, with a notation,
a few words scrawled in the margins
of the forest green class record book.
Something about the origin of composing,
a stray thought on effective
rhetoric. A speck, really.
Enough to make the eye blink and water.
A notion that all isn't right
in the classroom, where boredom
tussles daily with vertigo,
where individual cognitions occur
as rarely as the discovery of new planets.
Vita brevis, baby, you tell yourself,
don't fret on what you can't change,
but of course that doesn't assuage
the heavy throb of dissatisfaction.
Through the window you can see them
outside, murmuring and huffing smoke.
There must be some way to connect,
some conjuring trick beyond the constraints
of situational context. The books
are full of suggestions, rippling
with theory, cascading

> with what ought to be kick-
> butt kairos, but sometimes logic
> isn't enough. If it's a symbolic world,
> it's also a world of fumbling
> with buttons in icy brittleness.
> The art of pedagogy is learning
> how to span the breach between
> the taste of coffee, and those words,
> "the taste of coffee," in quotation marks.

The poem, or story, or piece of creative nonfiction about composing can be difficult to write. Wendy Bishop and I both knew that when we accepted Ken Autrey's invitation to join a panel called "Poems and Poets on Composing" that he proposed for the 1999 College Composition and Communication Conference in Atlanta. Yet for me, at any rate, this difficulty was one of the reasons I was interested in Ken's idea. I wanted to take stock of the dozens of poems I'd written about writing over the past decade, to sum them up.

I noticed immediately, as I sifted through my many failures, that it's hard to play it straight, to convey information about the composing process without sounding pedantic or grandiloquent. And the rules are different. In the lines above, for instance, I talk about "effective rhetoric. A speck, really." The positioning of those words is governed at least as much by my desire to emphasize their alliteration as by any other consideration. The imperatives of prosody, in other words, may supersede those of explanation, and that does, indeed, happen again and again in the many fine pieces in this book. Whatever claims might be made for *In Praise of Pedagogy*, it should be clear that the work here cannot be read the same way we read an article in *College Composition and Communication*, for instance, or *The Rhetoric Review*. Our poems and flash fictions and essays are overnight bags rather than steamer trunks. We pack them more cautiously, excluding everything but the absolute essentials.

Of course this is "just" an analogy, but it should remind us how dependent every theory of writing is on at least one central trope. Because poetry, especially, relies so heavily on metaphor, poems on composing—in comparison with expository prose on the same subject—are both richer in their evocations and more prone to the inaccuracies inherent in figurative language. The elision and compression that poetry and flash fictions and essays demand leads to implication rather than statement, aphorism rather than exposition. Frankly, many of the pieces in this collection allow the writer to circumvent a good deal of leg work; instead, they make you, the reader, "span the breach" yourself.

In the following poem, for instance, I "instruct" through in- and misdirection, through allusion and implication. Yet while my advice about how to write a poem is in some respects ironic, it is also sincere. I employ a diction that I wouldn't use if I were talking to a classroom full of students. I don't, however, suggest any guidelines that I wouldn't want my students to follow.

Instructions for Composing a Haiku

Make it exact: the ribs should show,
firm hoops beneath a thin shield of flesh.
It should sparkle like the skill
of a fastidious artist, precise
as a gnat. It should be a vessel
that requires nothing more than itself
to be full. A footstool. Quick.
A dagger. Microscopic.

Yet make it subdued, as the beginning or conclusion
of a rash. Let it melt
into shade, let it glide *toward* becoming
the way tides suggest something
about the shoreline that would otherwise
go unrecognized.

Granted, brevity and novelty
are its chief merits.
So above all it should shock
like the backward roll of thunder
in an unexpected gale.

Worried they'll see through it,
the knaves and hags? Worried

they'll toss it like dry straw onto a trash fire?
Don't worry: call it a frigate and name it
after a state. Conviction propels.
If they think it's seaworthy,
it'll float,
      goddamnit,
              it will float.

Of course any time a writer becomes emphatic—"it'll float, / goddamnit, / it will float"—we know he may be concerned about a potential weakness in the argument he's making. For me, at least, conviction doesn't always propel when it comes to the poem on composing.

Let me explain. In graduate school, in the MFA program where I completed a degree that has come to seem to me alternately liberating and, at times, "terminal" in more ways than one, I was told that the most boring art one could make was art about an artist making art. Both teachers and fellow students warned me that metafiction and poetry demonstrated a lack of imagination, a failure to connect with "real" people and "real" events. In the program where I studied—and I suspect this is still true of most graduate writing programs, whether they are oriented toward creative or critical or expository writing—there were fewer fates worse than being pigeonholed as someone who focused exclusively on the self while neglecting the larger society in which he was writing. Moreover, as I began submitting my work to literary magazines, I found this bias against the poem on composing confirmed by editors, many of whom were themselves writing teachers or students. The irony, of course, was that the one subject I most needed to learn about as an aspiring poet was made off-limits to my investigation.

In retrospect, I shouldn't have found this entirely surprising. While the work of the three and four Cs has been to demystify the writing process, this work has often been done in the face of implicit or outright scorn from the creative writing community. Too many belletristic writers still see themselves as artistés, creatures not subject to the normal laws of humanity.

Clearly, it is in the best interest of these people for the composing process to remain enigmatic.

Nevertheless, I continued to write the occasional poem about writing, although my own concerns as a graduate student writer were often focused on less than ethereal matters, such as making sure that my two children were adequately housed, clothed and fed. Indeed, it struck me that there was a direct correspondence between parenting and writing poetry, as evidenced in the following poem, which my thesis director found particularly appalling.

Poems, Like Children

Little things, they are neither as good
nor as hard as we want them to be.
They are conceived quickly and carelessly,
after work, before falling asleep.
But they demand everything
and grow too fast, their lives
brazenly independent of our own.
Go away we shout eventually,
sick to death of their imperfections.
Yet later, when the silence
in the house splits our ears,
we want them back,
though they are indifferent to us
and our need to cherish them.

In defense of my teachers and fellow students and the literary magazine editors, I have to admit that there is a sort of metapoem I didn't like myself, even back then. Anyone who has ever taught a beginning creative writing class has encountered this poem. Its theme is "I Couldn't Think of Anything to Write About, So I Wrote About Having Nothing to Say." The poem usually takes the form of a kind of protocol analysis, with the student recording and commenting on her own struggles with the composing process. Typically, the speaker of the poem is up very late the night before she must hand in her work. She considers and dismisses any number of potential subjects, then, finally, exhausted and just at the point of giving up, she is thunderstruck by inspiration. Ten minutes later, the assignment is complete. Popular titles for the resulting poem include "Writer's Block" and "Surprise!"

In class the next day, as the poem is read aloud, the student author beams at her own cleverness. The other students are impressed, too; *they* never would have thought of writing on that topic. Maybe they will try it themselves. Meanwhile, I sit there aghast, thinking, *Not again!*

Finally, several years ago, this scenario had played itself out one too many times. I forbade the appearance of these poems in my class. All I could see was the last-minute nature of the thing, the student's lack of imagination, the predictability of the conceit.

Lately, though, I've begun to reconsider the wisdom of my prohibition. Although it often *looks* like a slacker's handiwork, the Surprise! poem may well represent an unskilled writer's early attempts at understanding what makes herself tick. Indeed, the poem may serve several important functions. It makes concrete a very abstract process. Usually it results in a functional (if mundane) metaphor for writing. It demonstrates that, in part, the composing process is one of sorting through and eliminating possible choices. And the poem shows us where our interests lie, and where they don't. It shows us our limitations. It lets us know where we've been going wrong.

In fact, come to think of it, I am guilty of at least one variation on the Writer's Block poem myself:

Buttons

For years, I've wanted to write a poem
    about the buttons my wife keeps in
a 1940s peanut butter jar.
    Various, latent with significance,
they're the sort of odd things I tend
    to scatter through my verse: some small
as tears, others big as a fifty-cent piece,
    inscribed with strange sayings—SPOLIA

> OPIMA, EQUIPEMENTS MILITAIRES—
>   covered with satin or China silk,
> black and brown and gray, of course,
>   but also carmine, maroon and apricot,
> sunflower, beryl, pistachio.
>   Each time my wife dug through the jar
> I'd try to fabricate a clever
>   metaphor, but for years nothing came.
> Until today, when I realized
>   the problem's not the tenor or
> the lack of vehicle: the problem
>   is the poet, who cannot sew.

At times, reading through the poems that were submitted to this book, I have felt that we writing teachers are like earthworms. It is an unlovely image, I know, but what I mean is that all this writing about writing is like a hard rain that flushes us from the dark soil where we normally live and work up to a surface that is both alien and distantly familiar. We have some vague ancestral memory of the sky, but we have to make sense of it all over again. I'm not sure how earthworms handle this epistemological upheaval, but *we* deal with it by writing.

The poems and stories and essays in *In Praise of Pedagogy* make me want to put down the book and write. This is the same impulse I have whenever I attend a conference on writing: the desire to do rather than discuss. I know I'm not alone, for in every meeting room where conscientious notes are being taken on yellow notepads, I always see someone hunched over, intently writing a poem. It's a natural urge, to respond not just to the speaker on the dais but also to the people in the audience—those who are listening carefully, or doodling, or nodding off.

An Elderly Woman Falls Asleep at a Poetry Reading

And those of us behind her
can't help but smile.
The forty-something poet
sitting next to me—lately

come to his powers as scribe
of the exotic locale
and significant event—
scribbles a note. "Good poem

for you," he digs,
and it's true. From my vantage,
every minor thing is lyrical:
the lace-trimmed dress

scattered with green roses, red-
dyed hair balding at the part.
Her drooping head recovers mid-
metaphor, then drops again,

the wide pink hat with its nosegay
of plastic roses slipping
from her lap like a sheet
of onionskin. Forty-something

snickers at the snoring.
The poet pauses, gestures
grandly. "And those of us
behind her," I begin.

    I think my own poems about composing are often either statements of faith in the act of writing, or laments that writing is never really enough. I would argue, for instance, that "An Elderly Woman Falls Asleep at a Poetry Reading," despite its aura of melancholy, is actually quite optimistic. The speaker believes that by writing a poem about the elderly woman, he can in some way defend her from the sarcasm of his friend, affirm her essential human dignity.
    The following poem, however, though its initial tone seems much lighter, has no trust in redemption. For if, in one sense, poems are invaluable as a means of asserting that there is good in the world, in another sense, they are absolutely without value. Everyone knows that poetry is the opposite of money. And yet all poets continue to hope that their writing will ultimately be worth something to someone. This poem grapples

with that problem by envisioning an alternate world in which
the rewards of poetry are financial rather than spiritual.

The Year My Poetry Became a Fad

It was the coup of a lifetime for a minor poet
like me the day Chuck Brister of Brister,
Schlack & Toille picked up a copy
of *The SoHo Literary Review* (circulation
five hundred plus) in a coffee shop
on the Upper West Side. What he saw
in my poem "Variations on a Phrase
by Kurt Cobain" that ignited his
particular genius for selling things
is for genius alone to explain. I
can only be grateful that, in his words,
"I gulped my latté like it was water
and headed back to the office,
an entire campaign already forming
by the time I left the cab." He found
my number, called. I quickly acquiesced.
The most my verse had ever paid
was a couple hundred contest bucks
and Chuck was talking tens of thousands.
Maybe, he insinuated, a great deal more.

That, of course, turned out to be the case.
The break-through product was the T-shirt
by Hilfiger, which read across the chest:
"Who's to say what seedy script..."
and on the back: "Providence will stage
for our benefit?" Then Chanel
brought out Poesis, "A Scent for Men,"
with the tag: "a fragrance as fresh
as his metaphors." The illustrated volume
of my poems (talking point from Chuck:
"Never, *never* refer to it as a comic book")
was such a hit that the movie deal
became inevitable. McDonald's
and Burger King went at each other
for promo rights, but we decided

to go with Taco Bell: the advance
was smaller, but they gave us unheard of
points. I still have the plastic cup
with my smiling caricature and the logo:
"He Claims to Have No Theory
of Fiction at All!" I still sleep
on the Pacific Coast "Enjambment" sheets
and eat off the Starkey Strophe earthenware,
available exclusively through Pier 1 Imports.

But fads are meant to rage, ransack
and vanish noiselessly. The movie bombed.
In a single fiscal year I was played out.
When it was over, I grew silent,
the way ex-heroes are said to do.
Loathe to go back to the petty
rewards of poetry, the lonely clicking
of fingertips on keys, the unimportant
satisfaction of choosing the proper word,
I invested heavily in risky stocks, and lost.
It was two years before I wrote another line,
and, until today, it's only been occasional
verse: commissioned birthday cards
for CEOs, a "hip" new line for Hallmark
that sold modestly and was dropped.
The moral is obvious, but there's more
to it than that. Money matters.
And when the New American Poet
like me is broke, there's nothing will fix
him up again short of loans unimaginably
large, far beyond any poet's reckoning.

So much for worldly gain.

But I don't want to finish on this rather bleak note. Instead, I'd like to brag, just a little, about the importance of *In Praise of Pedagogy* as a bridge between composition and creative writing and literature, three sub-disciplines in English studies that, whatever their rival allegiances, are all concerned with literature-making. If our definitions of literature vary, depending on where and how and why we're writing and whom we're

writing for, there is still a common story we can all learn from.
We need to pay close attention to what that story is telling us.

The Pedagogy of Art

Just this once, I will resist narrative.
The skinny teenage boy I see in my mind
yearns desperately to flee the Ouachita
Mountains of southeastern Oklahoma
and move to the big city where he can
become a stout baldheaded man
with handlebar mustaches who plays
Bach and Telemann and Buxtehude
in the Dallas Baroque Ensemble.
I'm sorry. He'll have to stay at home.

In a village thirty miles from Rome,
a young woman of twenty wants to chuck it
all and emigrate. Her father, the local
tailor, ducks out each evening from seven
to ten. He buys cartons of rubber gloves
which disappear pair by pair. She knows
if she can find a single sympathetic
listener, that's her ticket out. Her mouth
moves, but her voice is just a murmur.
My hands are pressed against my ears.

I've got bigger ontological fish
to fry than these two dim syntactic
creations. There are citational lines
to cross, identifying impulses
to detonate. All around me, radical
praxis is at play, closure is being
rejected, "realisms" are finding
themselves decommodified. Yet I stand
here between transcendence and immanence,
weighted down with accreted images:

She's made her way to the Lone Star State
and is settling down in a darkened

concert hall. Applause. A stout man takes
center stage, positions the antique
instrument between his legs and bows.
I swear to God she and he and I
are trying to ignore the music,
but there it is, *Alleluia*
Alleluia as her program
plainly states, *Gloria Deus.*

Contributors' Notes

Laura Apol teaches writing and children's literature at Michigan State University. Her poetry has appeared in a number of literary journals and anthologies. Her first book, *Falling Into Grace*, was recently published by the Dordt College Press and she is currently completing a second book of poems: *Reciting Each Scar*.

Ken Autrey directs the writing program at Francis Marion University in Florence, S.C. His work has appeared previously in *Poetry Northwest*, *The Chattahoochee Review*, *The Texas Review*, and other magazines.

Joseph H. Ball is an AP teacher at Staples High School in Westport, CT. "of parts of her" will be published in *Intimate Kisses*, Wendy Malts, ed. (2000).

Jane Barnes is a composition teacher at North Central College in Naperville, Illinois, and facilitator of the long-standing Thursday Night Writers' Workshop at Elgin Community College. These poems are her first published work.

Grace Bauer teaches creative writing at the University of Nebraska. Her most recent book is *The Women at the Well* (Portals Press).

Steven Bauer directs the creative writing program at Miami University in Oxford, OH; his children's book *The Strange and Wonderful Tale of Robert McDoodle* has just been published by Simon & Schuster.

Wendy Bishop teaches writing at Florida State University in Tallahassee. Her most recent book is *Thirteen Ways of Looking for a Poem: A Guide to Writing Poetry* (Longman, 2000).

Jacqueline Brice-Finch is Professor of Africana Literature at James Madison University where she is editor of *MaComère*, the journal of the Association of Caribbean Women Writers and Scholars.

Craig Challender teaches American literature and creative writing at Longwood College in Virginia, where he also directs a reading series. Linwood Publishers recently brought out his first book, *Familiar Things*.

Kelly Cherry's most recent books are *The Society of Friends: Stories* (U of Missouri, 1999) and *Death and Transfiguration: Poems* (L.S.U., 1997). Her nonfiction includes the autobiographical narrative *The Exiled Heart* (L.S.U., 1991) and *Writing the World*, essays about writing and the writing life (U of Missouri, 1995).

Cynthia Miller Coffel, presently a graduate student in Language, Literacy, and Culture at the University of Iowa, has taught English in Utah, Indiana, and upstate New York. Her most recent work, "Famous Mothers and Others: Notebook of a First-Year Teacher" appeared in the 1999 edition of *Willa*.

Devan Cook writes with her students at Boise State University; essays begun and largely written for her classes are forthcoming in *The Subject Is Reading* and *Red Rock Review*.

Stephen Corey is associate editor of *The Georgia Review* at The University of Georgia. The most recent of his seven collections of poems are *Mortal Fathers and Daughters* (Palanquin P, 1999) and *All These Lands You Call One Country* (U of Missouri P, 1992).

Trista Cornelius is at the inspiring beginning of her career as a writer and teacher of writing. With a Master's degree focusing on composition theory and writing, she is teaching advanced and beginning college composition at three Oregon schools: a private liberal arts and sciences university, a four-year urban university, and a community college.

Helen Degen Cohen teaches part-time for Roosevelt University, and was Artist-in-Education through the Illinois Arts Council. Recent publications: *Natural Bridge* (U of MO, St Louis), *The Poetry Porch* (online), *King Log* (online), "That Dark Poland, The Work of Helen Degen Cohen" in *Something of My Very Own to Say: American Women Writers of Polish Descent* (University of Columbia Press, 1997).

Phebe Davidson holds the G. L. Toole Chair in English at the University of South Carolina–Aiken, where she teaches and manages Palanquin Press. Her most recent books are *Dreameater: Poems* (Delaware Valley Poets, 1998) and *Conversations with the World: American Woman Poets and Their Work* (Trilogy Books, 1998).

Geraldine DeLuca directs the Freshman English program at Brooklyn College. Her short story "This Winter" appeared in *Brooklyn Review* and a personal essay "Song for Two Guitars" in *Voices in Italian-Americana*, 1996.

Brock Dethier, author of *The Composition Instructor's Survival Guide* (Boynton/Cook), teaches at Utah State University.

Marvin Diogenes is director of the University Composition Board at the University of Arizona, where he teaches composition, fiction writing, and the teaching of creative writing courses.

Skip Eisiminger, professor of English and Humanities at Clemson University, is the author of *Wordspinner* (1991) and *Nonprescription Medicine* (1995).

Darrell Fike is an Assistant Professor of English at Valdosta State University.

Katherine M. Fischer teaches writing and directs the Writing Lab at Clarke College in Dubuque, Iowa. Her poetry, essays, and short fiction appear in journals, magazines, and books, most recently "RiverRising" in *Heartlands* (Nancy Durham, ed. 1999) and "Alewives" in *Web Weavers* (Sibylle Gruber, ed., NCTE, 1999).

Alice George conducts workshops at local libraries, colleges, and the Ragdale Foundation while pursuing her MFA at The School of the Art Institute of Chicago. An Editor of *Rhino,* a literary annual and writers resource, Alice is also a member of The Divas; journals publishing her work in 1999–2000 are *Quarter After Eight* and *Another Chicago Magazine*.

Douglas Goetsch teaches English and creative writing at Stuyvesant High School in New York City. He is author of two collections of poetry, *Nobody's Hell* (1999, Hanging Loose Press) and *Wherever You Want* (1997, Pavement Saw Press).

Melissa A. Goldthwaite is working on her Ph.D. in rhetoric and composition at The Ohio State University where she also teaches classes in composition, poetry, and creative nonfiction.

David Graham teaches at Ripon College and is the author of four collections of poetry, including *Second Wind*, an AWP Award Selection.

Ava Leavell Haymon conducts adult workshops in poetry writing and teaches students of all elementary and secondary grades through the Arts Council of Baton Rouge. Poems are published recently in *The Southern Review*, *The Sun*, *New Orleans Review*, and *Pennsylvania English*. Most recent chapbook: *Why the Groundhog Fears Her Shadow* (March Street Press).

Will Hochman is a professional writing tutor at St. Joseph College. His poetry has appeared in several collections and in over fifty magazines and journals. He is the poetry editor of *War, Literature & the Arts*.

Holly Iglesias coordinates Girls N Power, a program for low-income teenage girls that encourages empowerment through creative writing and reading books to younger girls. Her work has recently appeared in *The Prose Poem, Spoon River Poetry Review, The Women's Review of Books,* and a chapbook, *All That Echoes Her Large* (Permafrost). She is co-editor, with Catherine Reid, of *Every Woman I've Ever Loved: Lesbian Writers on Their Mothers.*

Allison Joseph is the author of three books of poems: *What Keeps Us Here* (Ampersand, 1992), *Soul Train* (Carnegie-Mellon, 1997), and *In Every Seam* (Pittsburgh, 1997). She teaches at Southern Illinois University in Carbondale, Illinois.

Kathleen Kirk teaches literature and writing at DePaul University in Chicago and co-edits *Rhino,* a poetry annual. Recent work appears in *Callaloo, Quarter After Eight,* and *Spoon River Poetry Review.*

Gerald Locklin has taught at California State University since 1965. His most recent of nearly one hundred books is *Go West, Young Toad: Selected Writings* (Water Row Press, 1999).

Janet McCann has taught at Texas A&M since 1969. Her most recent book of poems is *Looking for Buddha in the Barbed-Wire Garden* (Avisson, 1996).

Shannon Marquez McGuire is a New Orleans native who teaches at L.S.U. Her poems appear in numerous journals and in *Immortelles: Poems of Life and Death by New Southern Writers.*

Claudia MonPere McIsaac teaches creative writing and composition at Santa Clara University. Her essay, "Flowers, Bones" appears in *Living on the Margins: Women Writers on Breast Cancer* (Persea Books, 1999) and recent poems appear in *Prairie Schooner, Calyx,* and *Puerto Del Sol.*

Dean Newman teaches American literature and writing when he feels like it and performs editing and desktop publishing duties at the Florida Department of Education in Tallahassee.

Anne-Marie Oomen is chairperson of the Creative Writing Division at Interlochen Arts Academy and author of two chapbooks of poetry, *Moniker* and *Seasons of the Sleeping Bear*.

Hans Ostrom is Professor of English at the University of Puget Sound in Tacoma, Washington, where he lives with his wife and son. His books include the novel *Three to Get Ready* and *Lives and Moments: An Introduction to Short Fiction*.

Robert Parham heads the Department of Languages, Literature, and Philosophy at Armstrong Atlantic State University in Savannah, GA. His chapbook, *What Part Motion Plays in the Equation of Love* appeared this year from Palanquin Press.

Diane Payne is teaching special education students at an elementary school this year. She has a novel coming out from Red Hen Press and has been published in numerous magazines.

Kara Provost directs the Writing Center and teaches writing and literature courses at Montserrat College of Art in Beverly, MA. She has published poetry, memoir, reviews and academic essays in a number of journals, including *Hurricane Alice*, *MELUS*, and *Oshkaabewis Journal*.

William M. Ramsey teaches English at Francis Marion University in Florence, S.C. His poetry has appeared in *Barbaric Yawp*, *Cumberland Poetry Review*, *Exquisite Corpse*, *Poetry Motel*, *South Carolina Review*, *Tar River Review*, and in numerous haiku magazines.

Bill Ransom's most recent books include *Learning the Ropes* (Utah State University Press) and *Burn* (Ace Science Fiction). He teaches at The Evergreen State College in Olympia, Washington.

Terry Rasmussen, who holds an MA in English from Iowa State University, teaches composition and directs the creative writing program at Casper College, in Casper, Wyoming.

Tom Romano teaches in the Department of Teacher Education in Oxford Ohio. He is the author of *Writing with Passion* (1995) and *Blending Genre, Altering Style* (2000).

Darrell g.h. Schramm directs the writing program and teaches at the University of San Francisco. His work appears in NCTE's *Reflective Activities*, *Journal x*, *Statement*, *The Harvard Gay and Lesbian Review*, and other journals.

Sarah Sloane is an associate professor who teaches in the English and Women's Studies programs at University of Puget Sound in Tacoma, Washington. Her hair is growing gray and she contemplates coloring it.

Leonora Smith lives and writes in East Lansing, where she teaches in the Department of American Thought and Language at Michigan State University.

William Snyder, Jr. teaches writing and literature at Concordia College, Moorhead, MN.

Kate Sontag teaches at the University of Wisconsin-Oshkosh. Recent work can be found in *Boomer Girls* (U. of Iowa Press), *Prairie Schooner*, *Blue Moon Review* (online), *Green Mountains Review*, *Amelia*, and *Cicada*.

Scott Simpson has taught high school and college English, speech, and drama in both Texas and Nebraska, and is currently Assistant Professor of English at Black Hills State University in Spearfish, S.D. He holds an MA in Curriculum and Instruction and a Ph.D. in English–Creative Writing, both from the University of Nebraska in Lincoln.

Michael Spooner is Director of the Utah State University Press.

David Starkey has published more than 250 poems in literary journals in the United States, Canada, Britain, Australia, and New Zealand. He teaches at North Central College in Naperville, Illinois, and in 1999 was Fulbright Professor of English at the University of Oulu, Finland.

Thomas Stein is the English/Writing Learning Specialist at Dickinson State University. He was the recipient of the 1999 Red Acres Poetry Prize, and his poems have appeared in *Pif Magazine* and *The Advocate.*

Larry Strauss teaches English at Middle College High School in South Central Los Angeles. His most recent novel, *Unfinished Business,* is a murder mystery set in and around a financially corrupt inner-city high school and school district.

Alison Townsend is an assistant professor of English and Creative Writing at the University of Wisconsin–Whitewater. Recent work appears in *Kalliope: A Journal of Women's Literature and Art* and *Boomer Girls* (University of Iowa Press, 1999).

Patricia Valdata most recentlly taught at Harford Community College in Bel Air, Maryland. Her novel, *Crosswind*, was published in 1997.

Doyle Wesley Walls currently chairs the English department at Pacific University in Forest Grove, Oregon. His recent work in the personal essay has been published in *Under the Sun* and *Black Dirt* and is forthcoming in *Writing on the Edge.*

Lynna Williams directs the creative writing program at Emory University and is the author of *Things Not Seen and Other Stories* (Little, Brown, 1992).

Jane Elkington Wohl is Associate Faculty in the Goddard College M.F.A in Writing Program in Plainfield, Vermont, and English Instructor at Sheridan College, Sheridan, Wyoming. She is also director of the Sheridan Young Writers Camp, which meets each summer in the Big Horn Mountains. Her work has been published in numerous small journals and anthologies, most recently in *Leaning into the Wind: Women Writing from the Heart of the West* and *Shore Stories*.

Angus Woodward is an assistant professor of English at Our Lady of the Lake College in Baton Rouge. His short stories have appeared most recently in *Habersham Review* and *Gulf Stream*.

Acknowledgments

Some of the works in this book have been previously published in journals and magazines; thanks for permission to reprint and to those editors who first shared these texts with their readers.

Autrey, Ken. "The Dream of Teaching" first appeared in *Out of Unknown Hands: Poems by South Carolina Teachers*. Columbia, SC: R. L. Bryan, 1990. "The Poet Meets His Class in the Chemistry Lab" first appeared in *Poetpourri*.

Bauer, Grace. "Geography Lessons" first appeared in *Nebraska Life*. "The Scholar" first appeared in *The Bridge*.

Bauer, Steven. "Intro to Poetry" first appeared in *Prairie Schooner* and in *Daylights Savings*.

Bishop, Wendy. "Jo'al" first appeared in *Teaching English in the Two Year College*, copyright © 1991 by the National Council of Teachers of English, and is reprinted by permission. "Cross-Cultural Genres" first appeared in *Tonantzin*. "Othering" first appeared in *Seneca Review*. "The True Story of Theme Heaven" first appeared in *Florida English Journal*. "Here in the New World" is to appear in *The Higginsville Reader*. "Homework" was part of a Palanquin Press pamphlet.

Cherry, Kelly. "Advice to a Young Poet" first appeared in *English Journal* and is copyright © 1995 by Kelly Cherry. "A Note About Allen Tate" is reprinted from *Writing the World* by Kelly Cherry by permission of the University of Missouri Press. Copyright © 1995 by Kelly Cherry.

Corey, Stephen. "Art Elective" and "Freshman Lit & Comp" were originally published in *Synchronized Swimming*. "To an Ex-Student, On Learning She Is a World Class Gymnast" first appeared in *The Last Magician*.

Dethier, Brock. "Adjunct" first appeared in *CS/FEN*, now *Composition Studies*.

Graham, David. "Just Guessing" first appeared in *Maine Times*. "Long Overdue Note" first appeared in *Sycamore Review*.

Haymon, Ava Leavell. "First Piano Teacher" is to be published in *Pennsylvania English*.

Iglesias, Holly. "A Reading" first appeared in *The Prose Poem: An International Journal*. "The Autobiography of Tulips" first appeared in *All That Echoes Her Large*. Fairbanks, Alaska: Permafrost, 1999. "Deep Blue" first appeared in *Green Mountain Review*.

Kirk, Kathleen. "Teaching in My Sleep," and "Open Letter to My Students" first appeared in *Indiana English*.

Parham, Robert. "Ignoring the Linguist" first appeared in the *Christian Science Monitor*.

Romano, Tom. "The Teacher" first appeared in *English Journal*, copyright © 1982 by the National Council of Teachers of English. Reprinted by permission.

Smith, Leonora. "Spatial Relations" and "Fish/Spring/Window" first appeared in a limited edition chapbook *Faculty X* (Years Press). "Fish/Spring/Window" also appeared in *College English*, copyright © 1989 by the National Council of Teachers of English, and is reprinted by permission.

Snyder, William. "There Are Miracles Extant in This World" was first published in *Writing on the Edge*.

Starkey, David. "Instructions for Composing a Haiku" first appeared in *American Scholar*. "The Pedagogy of Art" first appeared in *Mangrove*.

Walls, Doyle Wesley. "X" first appeared in *Cimarron Review* and is reprinted here with the permission of the Board of Regents for Oklahoma State University, holders of the copyright.